We Believe

Transformative Truth for a
Life of Worship and Mission

EVERY NATION
R E S O U R C E S

Library of Congress Cataloging-in-Publication Data:
Title: We Believe: Transformative Truth for a life of Worship and Mission
Subject: Christianity | Theology
Print ISBN: 978-0-9854068-1-3

Images:
page 2 – Nicene Icon by unknown artist. Public Domain. Cropped from original. **page 9** – Joachim Neander (1650-1680) by unknown artist. Public Domain. **page 9** – Catherine Winkworth photo by unknown artist. Public Domain. **page 12** – *John Wycliffe reading his translation of the Bible to John of Gaunt* by Ford Madox Brown. Public Domain. Cropped from original. **page 19** – Portrait of Russell Kelso Carter by unknown artist. Public Domain. Cropped from original. **page 22** – Photograph of Abraham Kuyper. Public Domain. Cropped from original. **page 29** – Photograph of Cecil F. H. Alexander. Public Domain. Cropped from original. **page 32** – Icon of Irenaeus by Christos N. Liondas, licensed under Creative Commons. Cropped from original. **page 39** – The 'Lily Portrait' of a young Charles Wesley by unknown artist. Public Domain. Cropped from original. **page 42** – *Luther Before the Diet of Worms* by Anton von Werner. Public Domain. Cropped from original. **page 49** – *Isaac Watts* by unknown artist. Public Domain. **page 52** – *Catherine Booth: A Sketch* by Brigadier Mildred Duff. Public Domain. Cropped from original. **page 59** – Portrait of Augustus Montague Toplady by unknown artist. Public Domain. Cropped from original. **page 62** — Photograph of William Seymour by unknown artist. Public Domain. **page 62** – Photograph of The Apostolic Faith Mission on Azusa Street by unknown artist. Public Domain. **page 72** – Painting of Francis Asbury by John Paradise. Public Domain. **page 79** – Photo of Charles Hutchinson Gabriel by Jacob Henry Hall. Public Domain. **page 82** – Portrait of Augustine by unknown artist. Public Domain. Cropped from original. **page 89** – Photograph of Samuel Stone. Public Domain. **page 92** – Portrait of John Calvin by unknown artist. Public Domain. Cropped from original. **page 92** – Title page from the final edition of *Institutio Christiane Religionis*. Public Domain. **page 99** – Photograph of Dr. Timothy Tingfang Liu. Public Domain. **page 102** – John Wesley preaching on his fathers grave: in the church yard at Epworth Sunday, June 6 1742. Public Domain. Cropped from original. **page 109** – Portrait of Phoebe Worrall Palmer by unknown artist. Public Domain. Cropped from original. **page 112** – Icon of Second Coming by unknown artist. Public Domain. **page 119** – Photograph of the Fisk Jubilee Singers, 1875. Public Domain.

We Believe

Transformative Truth for a
Life of Worship and Mission

EVERY NATION
R E S O U R C E S

CONTENTS

Missional, Relational & Theological

"Mission brings us together. Relationships keep us together." That's my paraphrase of an oft-repeated saying that my good friend and longtime colleague Russ Austin uses to explain Every Nation.[1] From its founding, Every Nation has been a relational and missional movement. Relational because it started when two friends (Rice Broocks and Phil Bonasso) visited another friend in Manila (that's me). Missional because during that stop in Manila, the three of us joined our ministries to do church planting, campus ministry, and global mission together.

As crucial as mission and relationships have been in shaping Every Nation Churches & Ministries for over three decades, a third ingredient is equally important: theology.

Mission brings us together.

Relationships keep us together.

Theology strengthens us together.

We Believe: Transformative Truth for a Life of Worship and Mission is designed to strengthen our faith and deepen our theology as we study God's Word together.

While we have always valued sound theology in Every Nation, we tend to talk and write more about mission and relationships. Our missional/relational emphasis sets us apart from popular theological movements that emphasize one historical viewpoint. Theology brings these movements together and holds them together, with or without functional relationships or a compelling

---

1 — Here's the official Russ Austin version: "The mission brings us into relationships; our relationships sustain us for the mission."

mission. Sometimes they have relationships and do mission. Sometimes not so much.

We believe healthy relationships, global mission, and sound theology are all equally essential. Remove one, and we cease to be who God called us to be. Maybe not instantly, but eventually.

In Every Nation, you will find both Wesleyan and Calvinist pastors. You will also find a variety of eschatological opinions being espoused by complementarian and egalitarian preachers. If you listen to enough sermons, you might even discern that we have Pentecostals, charismatics, and third wavers. What you will not find are nontrinitarians, cessationists, and universalists.

When Every Nation started, the three founders were crystal clear that our mission was "church planting, campus ministry, and world mission," and we were to do it together. Mission. Relationship. That was clear. Since we assumed we were on the same page theologically, there were no doctrinal discussions.

As time went by and Every Nation expanded worldwide, we faithfully fulfilled our mission and worked on our relationships. However, we eventually found the need to clarify our core doctrines. Doctrines unify or divide and make room for some people and positions but not others. If a person disagrees with the essentials, the posi-tions codified in the statement of faith should cause a healthy separation.

In the beginning, we simply listed three historic creeds on our website under the "What We Believe" tab: Apostles' Creed (AD 215), Nicene Creed (AD 381), and Chalcedonian Creed (AD 451). After a few years, we added the World Evangelical Alliance Statement of Faith to the list of historical creeds. These creeds and statements served us well for our first fifteen years.

I clearly remember the moment I realized we needed to deepen the theological foundations of our global pastors and preachers. I was in Dubai at a regional leadership gathering, listening to mind-blowing mission reports from non-Christian cultures. Young men and women were hearing the gospel, lives were being transformed, and churches were emerging. Due to religious restrictions, missionaries could not secure visas and had to return home. As a result, relatively new Christians were now serving as pastors in several majority Muslim and Hindu nations. These pastors were saved, filled with the Holy Spirit, and doing a great job. They also had little theological training and were constantly seeking answers to common but tough theological questions.

This need led to a project called Leadership 215 (L215), based on 2 Timothy 2:15. Our goal was to create a course that would equip global ministers to do their best "to present yourself to God as one approved, a worker who has no need to be ashamed, rightly handling the word of truth." L215 became the minimum global theological standard for ordained ministers in Every Nation. With over 200 cohorts in more than 40 nations, over 2,000 leaders have received excellent theological training at no cost to them.

Many graduates of L215 felt the need to pursue accredited theological training and enrolled in seminaries all over the world, for better and worse. Some returned as better disciples, preachers, missionaries, and leaders. Others returned as hardened sectarians, extreme mystics, or critical know-it-alls.

A trusted and highly educated consultant dropped a wisdom bomb on me in 2016. "For a movement to survive and thrive beyond its founders, it must have its own songs and seminary. You cannot continue to outsource your music and theological education." At that time, Every Nation Music was just starting, but I had no desire to attend or start a seminary. Still, I went back to school, and now I'm a professor of Pastoral Theology at Every Nation

Seminary (ENS).

During the launch phase of ENS, we realized we needed our own statement of faith to guide our course developers and professors. They needed to know the Every Nation doctrinal boundary lines. We appointed a team of ENS theologians, historians, and Bible scholars to meet this need. Their work resulted in a 12-point ENS statement of faith that proved helpful for our course developers and professors.

The Every Nation Apostolic Council soon adopted the resulting ENS statement of faith as the overall Every Nation global statement of faith.

We Believe: Transformative Truth for a Life of Worship and Mission came from our 12-point statement of faith. As a result, our leaders now have a tool we believe will help us do life and mission together.

We owe a debt of gratitude to the team responsible for writing the Every Nation statement of faith and *We Believe*: Paul Barker, Bruce Fidler, Tom Jackson, and William Murrell.

May *We Believe* remind you that global mission brings us together, healthy relationships keep us together, and sound theology strengthens us together.

Steve Murrell
Cofounder and President of Every Nation

Why this book?

Why should we commit our time and energy to learn the doctrine in our Statement of Faith?

The answer to that question is summarized in the title.

We — We discover truth in community. God did not create us as isolated beings but as people in relationships with others. *We Believe* offers us the chance to grow in a communal setting.

Believe — Doctrine is an organized way to teach and learn the Bible. Therefore, studying it is not outdated or irrelevant because it matters what we believe. It will shape how we live, what we say to nonbelievers, and how we interact with the contemporary world.

Transformative — The primary goal of doctrinal study is personal change. Doctrine is an organized presentation of God's Word, and his Word is how he transforms us into his image. It is the primary agent of change in our lives. Doctrine is not dry and dull but living and dynamic.

Truth — Truth never changes, but it is emphasized and challenged in different eras. In this material, we will interact with God's truth as men and women throughout church history have emphasized and defended it. This will press our roots deep into the unshakeable realities of the gospel.

Life — Doctrine will first change the way we believe. Then it will change our hearts. And ultimately it will change the way we live. Our life will be dramatically impacted by a deep study of God's truth.

Worship — The first result of an in-depth study of God's Word is a greater love for him. A greater understanding of God's Word will produce a greater desire to worship him in all of life.

Mission — The second result of an in-depth study of God's Word is a greater love for people. A greater understanding of God's Word will produce a greater desire to proclaim him in all of life.

It is our prayer that this material transforms your life so that you will worship God better and fulfill his mission more effectively.

All Scripture is breathed out by God and profitable for teaching, for reproof, for correction, and for training in righteousness, that the man of God may be complete, equipped for every good work.

2 TIMOTHY 3:16–17

CHAPTER 1

The Doctrine of
God

We praise you, O God and acclaim you as Lord. All creation worships you, the Father everlasting. To you all angels, all the powers of heaven, the cherubim and seraphim, sing in endless praise: Holy, holy, holy Lord, God of power and might, heaven and earth are full of your glory. The glorious company of apostles praises you. The noble fellowship of prophets praises you. The white-robed army of martyrs praises you. Throughout the world, the holy Church acclaims you: Father, of majesty unbounded, your true and only Son, worthy of all praise, the Holy Spirit, advocate and guide. Day by day, we magnify you, and we worship your Name. O Lord, keep us this day without sin. Have mercy upon us, for our trust is in you.[1]

---

1 — Adapted from the *Te Deum Laudamus*, a fourth-century Latin prayer of uncertain authorship.

In his book, *Christian Theology*, Millard Erickson said, "The doctrine of God is the central point of theology. One's view of God . . . suppl[ies] the whole framework within which one's theology is constructed and life is lived."[1] That is why we begin with the doctrine of God on our journey to discover transformative truth for a life of mission and worship.

The Bible begins with a revelation of God the Creator (Genesis 1:1) and ends with him reigning on the exalted throne of the universe (Revelation 22:3). Between these two points, he reveals himself on every page.

The early Church Fathers spent much of their time studying and writing about the doctrine of God they found in the Scriptures. They faced many challenges from heretical sects which distorted essential truths about God. Through their struggles, they help form the basic ideas that the Church has held for centuries. Three friends from the geographical region of Cappadocia (modern Turkey) were significant in this process. We refer to them as the Cappadocian Fathers.

Icon depicting Constantine I, accompanied by the bishops of the First Council of Nicaea (325), holding the Niceno-Constantinopolitan Creed of 381.

The Cappadocian Fathers

In 318, the heretic Arius challenged the church's teachings on the Trinity. He taught that the Son was like God, but not the same essence as God. "If the Father begat the Son, then he who was begotten had a beginning in existence, and from this it follows there was a time when the Son was not." This was an attack on the foundation of Christianity.

Arius promoted his ideas with catchy songs and soon had a large following. When the controversy escalated to bloodshed, the emperor Constantine ordered 1,800 bishops to convene in Nicaea, but only 318 arrived. The Council excommunicated Arius and developed what we now know as the Nicene Creed.

But the Council of Nicaea did not resolve the Arian controversy. After Constantine's death, his sons and succeeding emperors supported Arianism and made it the orthodox faith of the State. Many bishops also embraced Arianism and rejected the teachings of Nicaea.

In response to the Arian heresy, three men from the region of Cappadocia, Basil of Caesarea (330–379), his brother, Gregory of Nyssa (332–395), and their friend Gregory of Nazianzus (329–389) produced the most articulate, biblically grounded, and philosophically-informed arguments for a pro-Nicene understanding of the Trinity. Their brilliant writing and eloquent oration firmly entrenched the doctrines of the Trinity, the deity of Christ, and the deity of the Holy Spirit in the church's life.

Each of the three scholars made a different contribution. Basil was the man of action who established a Christian community committed to the pursuit of the gospel and assisting the poor. Gregory of Nyssa was the scholar who created much of the theological terminology through his persuasive writing. And Gregory of Nazianzus was the orator who publicly championed the Nicene orthodoxy.

Together, their contributions led to the triumph of the Nicene faith at the Council of Constantinople in 381, establishing the orthodox doctrine of God and restoring unity in the church.

---

1 — Millard J. Erickson, *Christian Theology*, (Grand Rapids: Baker, 1993), 263.

What do we believe about God?

We believe *in one God, creator and sustainer of all things. He is perfect and unchanging; completely loving, good, and holy; limitless in knowledge, power, and presence. God eternally exists in three persons: Father, Son, and Holy Spirit; one in essence, having the same divine attributes and perfections, with each person fulfilling distinct roles. Gracious in his eternal purpose to redeem a people for himself, God is worthy of wholehearted love and worship.*

1. God is great.

There is none like you, O Lord; you are great, and your name is great in might. **JEREMIAH 10:6**

Theologians have placed God's characteristics into two categories: those he shares with humans (e.g., love, kindness, etc.) and those he does not (e.g., infinity, omniscience, etc.). We group the first set of attributes under the heading "the goodness of God." We group the second set under the heading "the greatness of God." They are attributes of God's being or essential nature. Theologians often call these "incommunicable attributes" because God does not have these in common with man.

When we say God is great, we mean that his attributes of greatness make him "wholly other" than us. He is so far above us we could never know him or be like him unless he revealed himself to us. He is all-powerful, all-knowing, unchangeable, and sovereign. He is self-existent and ever-present, infinite and eternal. We do not share any of these attributes. We have limited power and knowledge.

> *When we say God is great, we mean that his attributes of greatness make him "wholly other" than us.*

We are constantly changing. We are death-doomed. We had a beginning. There was a time when we were not, but God has always been.

This is the God Jeremiah contrasts with idols in our text. He says these idols are the work of men's hands; they are stupid and foolish, and Jehovah is qualitatively different from them. He is the living and true God and the everlasting King. He is the God who made the earth by his power and preserves it by his wisdom. He stretched out the heavens with his understanding. He speaks in the thunder, and the heavens roar with rain. He causes the clouds to rise over the earth. He sends the lightning with the rain and releases the wind from his storehouses.

Because God is great, he is greatly to be praised and we should declare his mighty works from generation to generation (Psalm 145:3–4).

2. God is good.

The Lord passed before him and proclaimed, "The Lord, a God merciful and gracious, slow to anger, and abounding in steadfast love and faithfulness, keeping steadfast love for thousands, forgiving iniquity and transgression and sin, but who will by no means clear the guilty, visiting the iniquity of the fathers on the children and the children's children, to the third and the fourth generation."
EXODUS 34:6–7

When we say God is good, we refer to the many attributes that humans share with him because he made us in his image. We can never be self-existent, all-knowing, or sovereign—attributes of his greatness. But we can be kind, just, and merciful. Those are attributes of his goodness.

God's attributes of goodness are moral attributes. They are attributes of his character. We call them "communicable attributes" because God has them in common with us. But God's attributes are perfect, and ours are a dim reflection marred by sin. God cannot improve or increase his attributes of goodness because that would assume they were not wholly perfect before. But we can and must increase these attributes in our lives.

One way we do that is through a revelation of his goodness, as we see in our text. The setting is a crucial time in Israel's history. The people have rebelled against the Lord, and he wants to remove them and start over with Moses. Moses intercedes for the people, and God agrees to accompany them to the Promised Land. Then Moses prays, "Please show me your glory." And God replies, "I will make all my goodness pass before you and will proclaim before you my name."

The listed attributes of mercy, graciousness, patience, love, faithfulness, forgiveness, justice, and wrath, summarize God's goodness. Scripture repeats the attributes in this list many times: Numbers 14:18-19; Nehemiah 9:17; Psalms 86:15; 103:8-10; and Joel 2:13. The frequency informs us how vital they are to us. As we meditate upon these attributes of God's goodness, we will become more like him daily. As the apostle said, "And we all, with unveiled face, beholding the glory of the Lord, are being transformed into the same image from one degree of glory to another" (2 Corinthians 3:18).

3. God is one.

Hear, O Israel: The Lord our God, the Lord is one. **DEUTERONOMY 6:4**

This is a difficult passage, and many English Bibles include a footnote with alternative translations. Some of the choices are, "The Lord our God is one Lord," "The Lord our God is the only true God," and "The Lord is our God, the Lord alone." All these options have in common the idea of one God.

This is monotheism, the belief that there is just one God. Monotheism is different from Polytheism, the belief in many gods; Pantheism, the belief that everything is god; and Atheism, the belief that there is no god.

Monotheistic belief is common today because of the prevalence of Judaism, Christianity, and Islam, but it was rare in the world of ancient Israel. The idea of one indivisible, all-powerful God was incomprehensible to the ancients.

That is what made Israel's faith unique and revolutionary.

In Romans, Paul argues that our first parents had been monotheists. Polytheism developed as the result of their rebellion. It grew as their offspring increasingly refused to honor God or give him thanks. Their thinking became futile, their hearts darkened, and they exchanged the glory of God for images resembling mortal man, birds, animals, and creeping things (Romans 1:21-23).

But when men rejected monotheism, they also rejected the foundation for ethics. If there is one God, then there is one absolute standard of right and wrong. But if there are multiple gods, there are multiple divine wills and, therefore, standards of right and wrong. This allows people to choose the one that best fits their predetermined moral choices or cultural preferences.

The prophet Malachi confirmed this when he appealed to monotheism in his prophetic denunciation of Israel's sin and injustice: "Have we not all one Father? Has not one God created us" (Malachi 2:10)? Monotheism created an ethical revolution that changed the world.

4. God is triune.

> Peter, an apostle of Jesus Christ, to those who are elect exiles of the Dispersion in Pontus, Galatia, Cappadocia, Asia, and Bithynia, according to the foreknowledge of God the Father, in the sanctification of the Spirit, for obedience to Jesus Christ and for sprinkling with his blood: May grace and peace be multiplied to you. **I PETER 1:1-2**

The doctrine of the Trinity teaches that God eternally exists as three persons, Father, Son, and Holy Spirit, and that each person is fully God, and that there is one God.[1]

The Trinity is one of the most challenging doctrines to comprehend because it transcends reason. However, the following three summary statements help us understand the Bible's teaching concerning the Trinity.

God is three persons.

When we say God is three persons, we mean that the Father is not the Son, the Son is not the Holy Spirit, and the Holy Spirit is not the Father. The Father, the Son, and the Holy Spirit can be recognized as different but cannot be divided in essence and relationship with one another.

Each person is fully God.

Each of the three persons has the same essence as God, and each possesses the fullness of God. Scripture consistently records that the Father, Son, and Holy Spirit have all the qualities of God.

There would be no logical problem with the Trinity if we ended here. We would assume that there were three Gods, all equal in power and authority. The third statement causes the intellectual problems associated with this doctrine.

There is only one God.

The three different persons of the Trinity are one in purpose and essence.

There are three primary things we learn from contemplating the Trinity.

- God is a relational, communal being within himself. And because he created us in his image, we were created for community. Nothing works right in our lives without it. A loving relationship with God and others is the ultimate meaning of life.

---

1 — Wayne Grudem, *Systematic Theology* (Leicester: Inter-Varsity Press, 1994), 226.

- God is unity with diversity. Therefore, we should strive for unity while embracing diversity. This is a model for us and a witness to the world.

- The Trinity is a mystery we will never fully understand. This should lead to awe and worship. The doctrine of the Trinity teaches us that we will forever worship God for his beauty and awesome splendor.

5. God is worthy.

> *"Worthy is the Lamb who was slain, to receive power and wealth and wisdom and might and honor and glory and blessing!"* **REVELATION 5:12**

In one of John's visions on Patmos, he sees and hears the heavenly choir shout seven things God is worthy to receive: power, wealth, wisdom, might, honor, glory, and blessing. The first six are intrinsic qualities of God, and the seventh is the creation's response to his worthiness.

God is worthy to receive power because he uses it for his glory and the well-being of his creation. He is worthy to receive wealth because, as the hymnist John W. Peterson wrote,

He owns the cattle on a thousand hills.
The wealth in every mine.
He owns the rivers and the rocks and rills.
The sun and stars that shine.

God is worthy to receive wisdom because among all the wise men of the nations and in all their kingdoms, there is none like him (Jeremiah 10:7).

He is worthy to receive might because he has made the heavens and the earth by his great power and outstretched arm, and nothing is too difficult for him (Jeremiah 32:17).

God is worthy to receive honor because he is the King of the ages, immortal, invisible, the only God, deserving honor forever and ever (1 Timothy 1:17). He is worthy to receive glory because he is the firstborn of the dead and the ruler of kings on earth. He loves us, freed us from our sins by his blood, and made us a kingdom and priests to his God and Father (Revelation 1:5–6).

Our response to God's worthiness is to sing to him and bless his name, tell of his salvation from day to day, and declare his glory among the nations and his marvelous works among all the peoples (Psalm 96:2–3).

MEMORY VERSE

"Worthy is the Lamb who was slain, to receive power and wealth and wisdom and might and honor and glory and blessing!" **REVELATION 5:12**

Application Questions

Which one of God's attributes of goodness (page 4) are you most deficient in? What practical steps can you take to be more like him in that area?

The Trinity teaches us community, diversity, and mystery. Which of these three is most applicable to your life? Why?

Which of God's attributes of greatness are the most significant to your current life situation? Why?

Pick one of the following attributes of God each day this week and meditate on it.

- **Immutable:** God never changes. *Malachi 3:6*
- **Omnipotent:** God is all powerful. *Psalm 33:6*
- **Omnipresent:** God is always everywhere. *Psalm 139:7–10*
- **Wisdom:** God is perfect in wisdom. *Romans 11:33*
- **Faithfulness:** God will never break his covenant. *Deuteronomy 7:9*
- **Just:** God is righteous in all his decrees. *Deuteronomy 32:4*
- **Merciful:** God is compassionate and kind. *Romans 9:15–16*
- **Gracious:** God is infinitely inclined to spare the guilty. *Psalm 145:8*
- **Holy:** God is perfect in his purity. *Isaiah 6:3*
- **Jealous:** God is passionate to protect what he values. *Ezekiel 39:25*
- **Sovereign:** God is in control of all things. *Daniel 4:34–35*
- **Providence:** God provides for his people. *Psalm 121:5–8*

Discussion Questions

What was your understanding of the Trinity in the environment you grew up in? Was a particular person of the Trinity emphasized more? How does that affect your devotional life now?

The Eastern branch of the historic church has tended to emphasize the oneness of God. The Western branch has tended to emphasize the three-ness of God. Which emphasis is easier for you to grasp? What are the potential dangers of emphasizing one aspect of God at the expense of the other?

What are the practical consequences of God's "otherness" in our lives, and how should a revelation of it change how we live?

Praise To the Lord The Almighty

Written by Joachim Neander
Translated to English by Catherine Winkworth

Praise to the Lord, the Almighty, the King of creation!
O my soul, praise him, for he is your health and salvation!
Come, all who hear; now to his temple draw near,
join me in glad adoration.

Praise to the Lord, above all things so wondrously reigning;
sheltering you under his wings, and so gently sustaining!
Have you not seen all that is needful has been
sent by his gracious ordaining?

Praise to the Lord, who will prosper your work and defend you;
surely his goodness and mercy shall daily attend you.
Ponder anew what the Almighty can do,
if with his love he befriends you.

Praise to the Lord! O let all that is in me adore him!
All that has life and breath, come now with praises before him.
Let the Amen sound from his people again;
gladly forever adore him.

Joachim Neander (1650-1680) was born in Bremen, Germany. He had a powerful conversion at age twenty and joined the German Reformed Church. He was ill most of his life and died at age thirty. But during the last years of his life, he drew great consolation communing with God in the beautiful Neandertal Valley of his home. He wrote many of his sixty hymns in a cave on the high rocky side of that valley.

Catherine Winkworth (1827-1878) was born in London but moved to Dresden, Germany, when she was eighteen. She spent a year there becoming fluent in the language and hymnody of Germany. Upon returning to England, she spent her life translating German hymns to English and establishing ministries to support women and the poor.

YouTube

Praise To the Lord, The Almighty (Live)
Victory Worship

CHAPTER 2

The Doctrine of
Scripture

Lord God, you have given us your Word for a light to shine upon our path. Let us keep it in mind and meditate on it day and night, persevering in prayer, always on watch. We beseech you, Lord, to give us real knowledge of what we read and show us how to understand it and put it into practice. May it give us wisdom. May it bring joy to our hearts and light to our eyes. May it instruct us in the fear of the Lord. May it guide us in the truth by the revelation of the Holy Spirit, through Jesus Christ our Lord, whose power and glory will endure throughout all ages. Amen.[1]

---

1 — Adapted from the prayers of Jerome (342–420), Origen (185–253), and the *Ancient Collects and Other Prayers* by William Bright.

The Bible is the most widely distributed book in history. It has been the primary agent for positive cultural transformation worldwide for nearly two thousand years. It was the foundation of Western culture, the bedrock of its educational system, and the inspiration for its literature, music, and art. No other book has had such a vast and formative effect on the history of the world as the Holy Bible.

Yet no other book in history has been more maligned, denounced, and vilified. For centuries, it has elicited the most defamatory attacks from intellectuals, skeptics, and critics. It seems that no one has been able to remain neutral about the Bible.

However, the Bible is more than just a shaper of cultures and a source of controversy; it is also our very life. Health, joy, peace, and true liberty abound within its pages. It gives wisdom beyond our years and health to our bodies. It provides a light to our feet and a lamp to our path. It is more precious than gold and more valuable than diamonds. It is the bread of heaven that nourishes and sustains us. It will make us fruitful in every venture as we study and meditate on it daily.

The Bible is the only written revelation God has given to man, and it is the final authority in all matters of faith and practice. All people need a copy of it in their language. John Wycliffe believed this and spent his life ensuring that God's Word would be available to the common speakers of English.

John Wycliffe

John Wycliffe (c. 1330-1384) was a highly-regarded professor and philosopher at Oxford University. His reputation began during his doctoral studies, when he gave a lengthy series of lectures commenting on the entire Bible. Trained in Hebrew and Greek, Wycliffe began criticizing numerous medieval church practices based on his study of Scripture. In his works *On the Church, On the Truthfulness of Scripture,* and *On the Power of the Pope* (1377-1378), he argued that the Bible

John Wycliffe reading his translation of the Bible to John of Gaunt.

was the only authoritative source for establishing Christian doctrine and no ecclesial authority had a right to add anything to it. Eventually, Oxford expelled Wycliffe and banned his books.

Undeterred, Wycliffe inspired others to join him in translating the Scriptures into the English language of his day. He was determined to make the Bible available to the common people so they might have direct access to its teachings. Working with Latin manuscripts, the group completed the New Testament in 1380 and the Old Testament in 1388, after his death. Wycliffe encouraged many volunteer lay preachers to distribute English copies of the Bible and spread his message of reform. These preachers became known as "Lollards," a derogatory term that mocked their lack of official academic education.

Wycliffe's influence lasted long after his death, spurring numerous movements to translate the Bible into the languages of the common people. Inspired by his example, the Wycliffe Global Alliance, a consortium of translation agencies, has a goal to translate the Bible into every world language. As of September 2022, the alliance was working on over 2,400 translation projects in at least 126 countries. More than 1,600 languages have translations of the New Testament, while more than 700 have the entire Bible. But their work is far from over because at least 1,680 languages still await the beginning of a Bible translation project.[1]

---

1 — https://www.wycliffe.org/

What do we believe about Scripture?

We believe *God has spoken through human authors in the Scriptures, the sixty-six canonical books of the Old and New Testaments. The Bible is the only written, verbally inspired Word of God and is self-attesting, unchanging, and without error in all it affirms. As God's authoritative, infallible, and sufficient revelation for life, doctrine, and practice, the Bible is to be trusted and obeyed.*

1. The Bible is God's inspired word.

> *All Scripture is breathed out by God and profitable for teaching, for reproof, for correction, and for training in righteousness, that the man of God may be complete, equipped for every good work.*
> **2 TIMOTHY 3:16–17**

While awaiting execution because of his faithfulness to Christ, the apostle Paul wrote these words to Timothy, his spiritual son and a church leader. Paul exhorted him to fulfill his divine calling to spread the good news of Jesus Christ and serve God's Church. To this end, Paul directed Timothy to the Scriptures, which then consisted of the same sacred Jewish texts known to us as the Old Testament. In addition, new documents were being written that testified to Jesus Christ and would become our New Testament, including the letter Paul wrote to Timothy. Together these documents comprise our Christian Bible.

The early church recognized the Holy Spirit inspired these texts. The writings were not merely an enlightened human witness to the living God but were documents produced by the Holy Spirit through participatory human authors. The Spirit superintended the transmission of his revelation

God continues to reveal himself through the biblical texts, which have enduring spiritual power.

through the human authors' own personalities and words so that the written words are truly the Word of God. The Holy Spirit worked through them to write texts that spoke to their intended recipients and those who would read the words in subsequent generations. God continues to reveal himself through the biblical texts, which have enduring spiritual power.

Paul's charge to Timothy included making disciples and developing leaders (2 Timothy 2:1-2). The Scriptures were necessary and useful for Timothy to equip others for every good work. In the same way, we need to give careful attention to God's revelation of himself throughout the sixty-six inspired books of the Bible. Through them, God speaks to us in many ways, including his promises and commands, which guide us and enable us to fulfill God's mission to make disciples and give us a sure hope that extends beyond this present life.

2. The Bible is authoritative.

> *For the word of God is living and active, sharper than any two-edged sword, piercing to the division of soul and of spirit, of joints and of marrow, and discerning the thoughts and intentions of the heart. And no creature is hidden from his sight, but all are naked and exposed to the eyes of him to whom we must give account.* **HEBREWS 4:12–13**

The writer of Hebrews was concerned that some of his fellow Jewish Christians were in danger of abandoning their faith and commitment to Jesus Christ. God had spoken to them about the great salvation freely offered to all who will trust Jesus and follow him. Jesus had suffered death on behalf of their sins, but it would not benefit them if they abandoned their faith. God's word is living and active, exposing the true disposition of the human heart toward God.

Because the Holy Spirit spoke through the human authors of Scripture, the Bible speaks with God's authority.

Because the Holy Spirit spoke through the human authors of Scripture, the Bible speaks with God's authority. It is more than the expression of human religious beliefs and values. It is the very word by which every person will be divinely judged, for God will summon all before his throne to give an account of their lives. The Spirit of God who inspired the Scriptures still speaks authoritatively through them today. His commands have not diminished with the passage of time but must be correctly understood and applied today. Those who wish to draw near to God must come before him in the reading and study of Scripture with reverence and humility.

God's authoritative word given to us as Scripture is good for our souls. It defines what is good and pleasing to God and what is evil and harmful to us. Our Creator knows and desires what is best for us, and the Bible speaks with authority to us in his promises and moral commands. His power, goodness, and integrity reassure us that he can be trusted and his rule is only always exercised in righteousness. Those who truly know him want to submit to him.

3. The Bible is trustworthy and without error in all it affirms.

> *Do your best to present yourself to God as one approved, a worker who has no need to be ashamed, rightly handling the word of truth.* **2 TIMOTHY 2:15**

Paul was willing to endure great suffering and even martyrdom for the sake of those who were being saved in Jesus Christ. He wrote from prison and urged Timothy to serve others by teaching them the truth of God's Word. Some had strayed from the truth and were teaching grave errors, upsetting the faith of some and leading them to ungodliness and ruin. Timothy needed to charge some to stop quarreling over words and avoid foolish, ignorant controversies. By diligently studying and teaching God's Word accurately, he could lead others in the truth and direct them to flee sin and pursue righteousness.

Because the Bible is divinely inspired, it is trustworthy in all it affirms. Understanding Scripture involves serious study, for its authors wrote in different historical-cultural contexts and languages from our own. When correctly interpreted, understood, and applied, it is thoroughly reliable as a source and a guide from the Holy Spirit. No one should shy away from reading and studying Scripture to avoid misinterpreting it because its central message and many of its great truths are understandable, even to a young child.

Each of us can learn to study the Bible more carefully. Most of us have access to more than one good translation of the Bible. We have teachers, books, and the accumulated wisdom of God's people from over three thousand years from which to learn. Therefore, we should apply ourselves diligently to know, understand, and apply God's Word to our lives and teach others to do the same. We can be sure that what we accurately learn in Scripture is dependable, for in it God is speaking to us, and he is faithful and true.

4. The Bible is sufficient for all we need.

> For whatever was written in former days was written for our instruction, that through endurance and through the encouragement of the Scriptures we might have hope. **ROMANS 15:4**

Paul wrote to the Roman Christians to help the Jewish and Gentile believers grow together in their salvation in Jesus Christ. Though their backgrounds and cultures were very different, Paul pointed them to the Scriptures to learn how to live and fulfill God's calling together. He believed the Scriptures were sufficient to guide all of God's people to live their lives worthy of the Lord Jesus and glorify God.

The Bible is adequately clear and sufficient to provide us with the knowledge necessary to have a relationship with God through Jesus Christ and to live a life pleasing to him. It is clear, understandable, and self-authenticating (i.e., it interprets itself—commonly expressed in the

If we abide in his Word, we will know the truth, and the truth will set us free.

statement "Scripture interprets Scripture"). The Bible doesn't answer every question we have but tells us what we need to know to walk with God. We should reject every so-called "revelation" that contradicts what is evident in the Bible and not be bound by any spiritual teaching that goes beyond Scripture. Likewise, we should never be dogmatic about biblically uncertain or unclear matters.

We should habitually read and study the Bible, relying on the Holy Spirit and the help of others. Over time we will grow in an understanding of God, his Church, this world, and our place in God's plan. If we abide in his Word, we will know the truth, and the truth will set us free.

5. The Bible is to be obeyed.

Whoever has my commandments and keeps them, he it is who loves me. And he who loves me will be loved by my Father, and I will love him and manifest myself to him. **JOHN 14:21**

Jesus spoke with his closest disciples the evening before his betrayal, arrest, and execution. He told them about the future with a deep love for them, reassuring them he would go before them to the Father in heaven. Yet, he would not leave them as orphans but would come to them again, sending the Holy Spirit to be with them to enable them to obey his commands. Though the disciples would face many hardships and dangers because of their commitment to him, he told them obedience to his commands was the true measure of their love for him. The one who does not love him does not obey his words.

Obedience to the clear teaching of Scripture is obedience to God. Jesus said if we keep his commands, we will abide in his love and be his friends. Those who keep even the least of God's commands and teach others to do the same will be called the greatest in God's kingdom.

God wants us to walk in a manner worthy of Jesus, fully pleasing him, bearing fruit in every good work, and growing in our knowledge of God. To do this, we must apply the Scriptures to our lives through the help of the Holy Spirit. Those who do this will build their lives on the rock. They will endure the storms of life and receive a rich welcome into God's eternal kingdom. Let each of us pray that God would renew our minds through Scripture and strengthen our hearts through the Holy Spirit so that we might obey everything he commands.

MEMORY VERSE

All Scripture is breathed out by God and profitable for teaching, for reproof, for correction, and for training in righteousness, that the man of God may be complete, equipped for every good work. **2 TIMOTHY 3:16–17**

Application Questions ✐

Do you have a time and place to read and study God's Word daily? What can you practically do to increase or enhance your study of Scripture?

How can you better use the Bible to address a contemporary issue?

How can you use Scripture more effectively when helping someone follow Jesus?

Create a list of five or more verses concerning the power of God's Word and confess them every day.

Discussion Questions

What is meant by the Christian claim that the Bible is divinely inspired?

|||||||||||||||||||||||||||||||||||||||||||||||||||||||||||||||||||||||||||||||||||

How do the Scriptures function authoritatively for Christians?

|||||||||||||||||||||||||||||||||||||||||||||||||||||||||||||||||||||||||||||||||||

How should we approach apparent difficulties or contradictions in Scripture?

Standing on the Promises of Christ My Savior

Written by Russell Kelso Carter

Standing on the promises of Christ my King,
through eternal ages let his praises ring—
"Glory in the highest," I will shout and sing,
standing on the promises of God.

Refrain:
Standing, standing, standing on the promises of Christ my Savior.
Standing, standing, I'm standing on the promises of God.

Standing on the promises that cannot fail,
When the howling storms of doubt and fear assail,
By the living Word of God I shall prevail,
Standing on the promises of God.

Standing on the promises of Christ the Lord,
Bound to him eternally by love's strong cord,
Overcoming daily with the Spirit's sword,
Standing on the promises of God.

Standing on the promises I cannot fall,
Listening every moment to the Spirit's call,
Resting in my Savior as my all in all,
Standing on the promises of God.

Russell Kelso Carter (1849–1928) became a Christian at fifteen in his parent's Presbyterian church. He trained for the military and graduated as a captain, later serving as a professor at the Pennsylvania Military Academy. But in 1872 he was forced to resign because of heart trouble. Three years later, when he was at the point of total collapse, God healed him through the ministry of Charles Cullis.

After another powerful encounter with God at a Methodist Revival, Carter became a devout proponent of divine healing. His theological writings laid the foundation for the healing ministries of early Pentecostalism and the Latter Day Rain movement.

Carter had a stormy life and career, revising his theological positions frequently, endorsing questionable medical devices, and severing important relationships (including divorcing his first wife). But his desire for God was a constant throughout his life and is reflected in his books and hymns.

He wrote "Standing on the Promises of Christ My Savior" in 1886.

YouTube

Standing on the Promises
The Acappella Company

CHAPTER 3

The Doctrine of Creation and Fall

OPENING PRAYER

The whole of creation declares your glory, Lord, and you reveal yourself in the everlasting fabric of the world. You are the God of heaven and earth, seas and rivers, sun and moon, and all the stars. The sun sings your praises, the moon gives you glory, and all creatures offer a hymn to you. Let all the trees of the forest dance and sing; let the mountains and hills break forth into rejoicing at your mercy, and let the trees of the forest clap their hands. Let everything that has breath praise and exalt you forever. Lead us, O God, from the sight of your beautiful creation to the thought of you, our Creator, and grant that by delighting in your creation, we will delight in you.[1]

1 — Adapted from the prayers of Patrick, Augustine, Clement of Rome, and the Eastern Orthodox Church.

God's story begins with creation. It is the first fact recorded in the Bible and the theological foundation for all that follows. It establishes the sovereign-personal Triune God at the center of the universe and reveals that everything and everyone is dependent upon and responsible to him. It reveals who man is and what eventually goes wrong in the story of redemption.

The fall is introduced in Genesis 3 and expanded through Genesis 11. There are hints of redemption in these chapters, but the primary role of this section is to detail the depth of evil in the human heart. Moses goes to great lengths to highlight just how sinful sin is. This is essential if we are to understand redemption. We can only know the greatness of his provision when we know the magnitude of our debt.

"Genesis lays the groundwork for all human ills in a fallen world: we are dislocated within ourselves, dislocated from each other, dislocated from God. Personal fragmentation, social tension, and spiritual alienation are now the parameters of life on earth."[1]

The theologian Abraham Kuyper spent much of his professional life considering the ramifications of the creation and fall.

Abraham Kuyper

Abraham Kuyper (1837–1920) was a Dutch theologian, journalist, pastor, prime minister, and university founder. His remarkable accomplishments in so many fields might make future historians wonder if there were several men named Abraham Kuyper who just happened to be alive simultaneously.

The son of a pastor, Kuyper studied theology at university and earned his doctorate in theology at the age of twenty-six. However, during his studies, Kuyper almost lost his faith. Ironically, his turning point came not while studying theology but when reading a novel about one man's spiritual transformation. This fictional character's transformation from a dishonest hypocrite to a virtuous man forced Kuyper to grapple with his pride and sinfulness, bringing him to the gospel's good news.

The central idea that transformed Kuyper and set the trajectory for the rest of his life was that God was the creator and sustainer "over the cosmos, in all its spheres and kingdoms, visible and invisible." While reflecting on Genesis 1–2, Kuyper was astounded that God had given humanity the task to steward and cultivate the "multiform world God had created." This meant that no sphere of society was beyond God's sovereignty; therefore, no sphere of society was off limits for Christian engagement.

Kuyper famously said, "There's not a square inch in the whole domain of human existence over which Christ, who is Lord over all, does not exclaim, 'Mine!'" This truth inspired Kuyper himself to engage in numerous spheres of Dutch society. For Kuyper, God was the creator—and the redeemer—of all things. And it was the calling of all Christians to participate in both creative and redemptive work to the glory of God.

Kuyper in 1905

1 —Alec Motyer, *Look to the Rock: An Old Testament Background to Our Understanding of Christ* (Grand Rapids: Kregel Publications, 1996), 119.

What do we believe about the creation and fall?

We believe *God created all things, visible and invisible, out of nothing, and all very good. He sovereignly sustains and governs creation for his glory and the benefit of his creatures. God created humans in his image, male and female, to know, love, and glorify him in covenant relationship and to serve as stewards of the earth. The first man, Adam, sinned against God, resulting in alienation, death, guilt, shame, and a curse upon the earth. Separated from God and subject to his judgment, all humans have inherited a sinful nature from which they cannot save themselves.*

1. God made all things good.

> *In the beginning, God created the heavens and the earth . . . And God saw everything that he had made, and behold, it was very good.* **GENESIS 1:1, 31**

At the foundation of the biblical story are two fundamental claims: God created all things, and all he created was good. The idea of one all-powerful God who created everything was not understood or believed in ancient cultures. They assumed there was a pantheon of gods who carried different levels of responsibility for creating and sustaining the cosmos and the creatures in it. The world, they believed, was the result of some cosmic conflict between warring deities. The created world was the result of violence. Therefore, the material world was evil—or, at best, neutral.

The biblical story proclaims something radically different and new: one all-powerful God created everything with intentionality and delight. Rather than wrestling with competing deities for supremacy, the God of the Bible is supreme. And rather than creating the world and its creatures through killing competitors, God creates through speaking and breathing life. Because of who created the world and how he did it, the biblical worldview claims that everything and everyone God made is good. This is stated repeatedly in the biblical account of creation in Genesis 1.

Even though most people today do not share the worldviews and creation myths of the ancient world, the claim that God made all things good is still countercultural. To embrace this claim today is to push back against the idea that the created world and its creatures were a cosmic accident—the chance result of chemical and physical processes. To embrace this claim today is to affirm that creaturely existence is neither meaningless nor accidental but rather full of purpose, goodness, and beauty.

That is why we must embrace the biblical doctrine of creation. Without it, there is no foundation for the great story of redemption that follows it.

2. God governs everything he made.

> *"You are the Lord, you alone. You have made heaven, the heaven of heavens, with all their host, the earth and all that is on it, the seas and all that is in them; and you preserve all of them; and the host of heaven worships you."* **NEHEMIAH 9:6**

It is significant to claim that God created all things, but it is not enough. The Bible goes much further, for it repeatedly declares that God governs and sustains everything he made. God could have created everything and then left the creation to manage itself. This is the fundamental idea behind Deism, an early modern worldview that assumes a divine creator who made the world and then left it alone to operate by the laws of nature. This is also often the operative view of many cultural Christians who acknowledge the existence of a divine creator but don't see a role for him in everyday life.

But the Bible paints a different picture. It displays a God intimately involved in his creation, governing all things according to his will and sustaining his creatures—great and small. This is the idea the writer of Nehemiah conveys in our text. He shows us a God who not only created the heavens, the sea, and the earth but also preserves and provides for the creatures he put there—birds, fish, animals, and of course, people.

Most ancient societies believed that the gods governed the earth and, as a result, acknowledged their dependence on the gods (or God) for rain, good crops, and material benefits. However, in our modern, urbanized, and scientific age, we are often insulated from our creaturely vulnerability and utter reliance on God's sustaining work in creation. Usually, it requires a natural (or man-made) disaster to remind modern humans that we are not lords of creation. God is. And that is fortunate because humanity does not have a good track record of governing itself and the earth.

3. God made humans in his image.

> *So God created man in His own image; in the image of God He created him; male and female He created them. Then God blessed them, and God said to them, "Be fruitful and multiply; fill the earth and subdue it; have dominion over the fish of the sea, over the birds of the air, and over every living thing that moves on the earth."* **GENESIS 1:27–28 NKJV**

What exactly does it mean that God made humans in his image? Clearly, the Genesis author is not referring to a physical resemblance—like children resembling their parents. Then what is he referring to?

The image of God (often referred to by its Latin name "Imago Dei") is first mentioned in Genesis and then expanded on by the other biblical authors. It means that man possesses characteristics that separate him from the rest of creation. These characteristics generally fit into the following five categories:

- **Intellectual:** Man is aware of self and can think, reason, and learn. He can communicate verbally using complex, abstract language. He has an innate creativity that manifests in art, music, literature, science, and technology. He can calculate and perform logical and analytical functions. He can design, create, and invent.

- **Ethical:** Man can distinguish between right and wrong. He can make real moral choices.

- **Emotional:** Man can feel anger, love, compassion, grief, and the entire range of human emotions.

- **Teleological:**[1] Man has a longing for purpose and responsibility. He has immortality; he will not cease to exist but will live forever. He has not only a physical body but also an immaterial spirit and can act in eternally significant ways.

- **Relational:** Man can have a relationship with God. This means he can relate to God, pray and praise him, and hear him speaking his words. He can develop relationships with other humans and experience community.

God created us to reflect his glory, to see the latent potentiality within creation, and "be fruitful and multiply." For example, only humans could cultivate wheat, mix it with water, salt, and heat, and make bread. Only humans, with our innate moral capacity, could orient our creative, culture-making work on earth toward the good of all creatures. Bread, for example, is meant to be shared to sustain human life. To see the creative potential in God's creation and to make something of it for the good of others is to bear his image on the earth and fill it with his glory.

4. Humans rebelled against God.

> *Then the Lord God called to Adam and said to him, "Where are you?" So he said, "I heard Your voice in the garden, and I was afraid because I was naked; and I hid myself." And He said, "Who told you that you were naked? Have you eaten from the tree of which I commanded you that you should not eat?"* **GENESIS 3:9–11 NKJV**

In the creation accounts of Genesis 1–2, we meet God as the supreme creator and sustainer of all things and of humanity made in his image with dominion on the earth. But the story quickly takes a catastrophic turn. God gave Adam and Eve great liberty in his Edenic Garden of Delight. He had only one law: Don't eat from the Tree of the Knowledge of Good and Evil. The tree represented God's authority, and when they ate of it, they rejected his authority. George Whitefield said about this event, "Alas! What a complication of crimes was there in this one single act of sin! Here is an utter disbelief of God's threatening; the utmost ingratitude to their Maker … Here was the utmost pride-of-heart: they wanted to be equal with God … the devil is credited and obeyed before him. Never was a crime of such a complicated nature committed by any here below: Nothing but the devil's apostasy and rebellion could equal it."[2]

What transpired at this moment of rebellion, and what does it mean? Two things are clear. First, Adam and Eve doubted God's goodness. Perhaps, as the serpent insinuated, God's command was not for their good. Perhaps, if they ate from the tree, they would transcend their creaturely status and become like God. This is always the root of human rebellion—our failure to trust God's word and character.

Second, humanity's rebellion had widespread consequences. For Adam and Eve, the results of disobedience manifested in their relationship with God, one another, and creation. This is how

---

1 — Teleological derives from the Greek word telos meaning end or purpose and logos meaning the study of something. Teleology is the study of ends and purposes. It assumes that life is heading somewhere rather than in meaningless circles.

2 — *Selected Sermons of George Whitefield*, "The Seed of the Woman, and the Seed of the Serpent," Christian Classics Ethereal Library, accessed April 20, 2023, https://ccel.org/ccel/whitefield/sermons/sermons.iii.html.

sin affects all humans. It separates us from God and people. It harms us and those around us. It infects our souls, institutions, communities, and ecosystems. It is like a deadly virus spreading in a densely populated city. It is like a toxic chemical poured into a river that spreads without limit and kills whatever it touches.

The story that began with such promise in Genesis 1 and 2 has in Genesis 3 plunged creation into a hopeless abyss. Only a new Adam can save it.

5. All humans are sinful.

> *There is none righteous, no, not one; There is none who understands; There is none who seeks after God. They have all turned aside; They have together become unprofitable; There is none who does good, no, not one.* **ROMANS 3:10–12 NKJV**

The consequences of Adam and Eve's rebellion extended far beyond their lifetime and homeland. The fall of humanity was not gradual but swift and violent. Adam and Eve's firstborn son, Cain, murdered his younger brother Abel. Cain's descendant, Lamech, boasted that he killed a man for wounding him and a mere boy for hurting him. His disregard for human life is matched by his disregard for the dignity of women expressed in his bigamy. Man's violence became so great that God sent universal judgment. But even the flood couldn't stop the pattern of sin. Noah's story begins with his righteous testimony and ends with him drunk in a degraded condition. The chronicle of man's sin then reached a new low when the Babel tower builders rebelled against God's command to fill the earth and rejected his sovereign right to rule their lives.

What is abundantly clear from the earliest pages of the Bible and any era of human history is that all humans are sinful. This is an empirical fact. The theological question is, "Why?" Throughout Scripture, we encounter the idea that we are not only sinful because we find ourselves in a hostile environment filled with sinful people and sinful systems. We are sinful because we have inherited that nature from our ancestors. Sin affects us not only from the outside in, but also from the inside out.

We call this "original sin." Though there are many ways to unpack and support this claim from Scripture, our own experience of life and human brokenness is enough to confirm the reality that something inside of each of us is bent and broken. We think thoughts we'd never want anyone to know. We want things we know are perverse. We do things we wish we could undo. We love in ways that are disordered and unhealthy. Though we are all made in the image of God, we know we don't look like him anymore. As Paul writes in Romans 3:10, "There is none righteous, no, not one." This search for a righteous one is the fundamental narrative thread of the Old Testament. When will he come, and from where? And how will we know him?

MEMORY VERSE

There is none righteous, no, not one; There is none who understands; There is none who seeks after God. They have all turned aside; They have together become unprofitable; There is none who does good, no, not one. **ROMANS 3:10–12 NKJV**

Application Questions

What is one consequence of original sin that you see is currently at work in your life? Why? What will you do to defeat it?

What are the practical implications of clearly understanding that God governs and sustains all things in your life? What would change if you were continually aware of those two things?

How has the devil tried to get you to doubt God's goodness in the past, and is there any way he is currently using the same strategy? What must you do to defeat him?

Meditate on God's creation: Read Psalm 19:1-6, then go to a quiet place where you can observe the natural world. Look and listen to God's creation for fifteen minutes without interruption. Focus on the sights and sounds you normally ignore and quietly commune with God, thanking him for the wonders of creation.

Lament human sin: Read Lamentations 1, then go to a quiet place and spend fifteen minutes reflecting on the disastrous effects of human sin on our world. You may go deep (reflecting on the implications of one particular sin in a particular place) or you may go wide (reflecting on many kinds of sins and injustices throughout the world). As you feel moved, pray for God's justice and restoration in those areas you have identified.

Discussion Questions

Why is it essential to have a worldview shaped by the biblical account of creation, and what are the results of denying the biblical account of creation?

Ⅱ||||||||||||||||||||||||||||||||||||||||||||||||||||||||||||||||||||||||||||

What is the image of God, and why does it matter that we believe and embrace it?

Ⅱ||||||||||||||||||||||||||||||||||||||||||||||||||||||||||||||||||||||||||||

What are the consequences of human rebellion in our relationship to God, others, and the creation?

All Things Bright and Beautiful

Written by Cecil Frances Alexander

Refrain:
All things bright and beautiful,
all creatures great and small,
all things wise and wonderful,
the Lord God made them all.

Each little flow'r that opens,
each little bird that sings,
God made their glowing colors,
God made their tiny wings.

[Refrain]

The purple-headed mountain,
the river running by,
the sunset, and the morning
that brightens up the sky;

[Refrain]

The cold wind in the winter,
the pleasant summer sun,
the ripe fruits in the garden,
God made them, ev'ry one.

[Refrain]

God gave us eyes to see them,
and lips that we might tell
how great is God Almighty,
who has made all things well.

[Refrain]

Cecil Frances Alexander (1818–1895) was born in Dublin, Ireland. In 1850, she married Reverend William Alexander, who later became the chief bishop of Ireland. She published nearly 400 hymns in her life, most written for children. This one was published in 1848. It elaborates on the Apostles' Creed and Psalm 104:24–25.

Alexander was deeply concerned for the poor and marginalized in society and used her influence to support charitable causes. She spent much of her time caring for the sick and regularly visited infirmaries and the terminally ill. She wrote many of her hymns to support charitable causes, especially educational support for the disadvantaged and the deaf and blind.

Besides the hymn "All Things Bright and Beautiful," she penned "Once in Royal David's City," a favorite Christmas hymn, and "There is a Green Hill Far Away" on the crucifixion of Jesus. Her hymns are deeply theological, poetic, and accessible to all.

YouTube
All Things Bright and Beautiful
Catholic Fellowship Jakarta

CHAPTER 4

The Doctrine of
Jesus

OPENING PRAYER

Jesus, you paid the debt of sin for us by your blood poured out in lovingkindness. You cleared away the darkness of sin by your magnificent and radiant resurrection. You broke the bonds of death and rose from the grave as a Conqueror. You reconciled heaven and earth. You overcame the sting of death and opened the kingdom of heaven to all believers. You are now seated at God's right hand in glory. We had no hope of eternal happiness before you redeemed us, but your resurrection has washed away our sins, restored our innocence, and brought us joy. [1]

---

1 — Adapted from the *Te Deum*, the *Liturgy of Gregory the Great* (540–604), and a fourth-century anonymous papyrus.

The study of the person and work of Jesus is vital because the truth about him is the foundation of Christianity (1 Corinthians 3:10–11). He is the focal point of the Bible; all the narratives point to him. Every part of the Bible bears witness to who Jesus is and what he came to do. On the Emmaus Road, Jesus taught his disciples that "Everything must be fulfilled that is written about me in the Law of Moses, the Prophets and the Psalms." These three main divisions of the Hebrew Scriptures imply that the entire Bible is about him. Therefore, if we are wrong about him, we will be wrong about all the other major themes of Scripture.

Without a proper understanding of who Jesus is, we cannot understand forgiveness, regeneration, or justification, and we cannot be saved. That is why the doctrine of Christ has been one of the most challenged doctrines in history. Heresies have abounded throughout the long story of the Church. Therefore, we must understand who Jesus was and is, and how that truth should apply to our lives.

The early church fathers understood this doctrine's importance and battled to lay the foundation for our current understanding. Irenaeus was one of those warriors.

Irenaeus

Irenaeus was born in Asia Minor around 130. He went as a missionary to Southern France and witnessed the persecution under the emperor Marcus Aurelius (177). When the Romans executed bishop Pothinus, Irenaeus succeeded him in that role. To fulfill his duty as bishop, he informed himself of Gnostic doctrines. He wrote *Against Heresies* around 180 to disprove the incorrect interpretations of Scripture and false teaching of the Gnostics.

Gnosticism was a Christian heresy with many different versions. The word comes from gnosis, the Greek word for knowledge. It was primarily

Icon of St. Irenaeus

a second and third-century heresy, but Paul and John addressed earlier forms of it in Colossians (c. 61) and John's gospel and epistles (c. 85–95).

The Gnostics taught that divine sparks had fallen from heaven into evil material human bodies. To unlock man's divinity and free him from the prison of the flesh required secret knowledge, imparted through initiation rites. Their primary tenet was a radical distinction between evil matter and pure spirit. A good God could not have created the evil material world; it was created by a lesser being usually associated with the God of the Old Testament. Because God was a pure spirit, he could not dwell in a human body. Therefore, Jesus was either not God, or he just appeared to have a material body.

Irenaeus contended that God made the natural world to be good and that sin and rebellion had perverted it. Christ came in the flesh to redeem mortal beings. He said, "Christ has summed up all things, both waging war against our enemy, and crushing him who had at the beginning led us away captives in Adam. As our species went down to death through a vanquished man, so we may ascend to life again through a victorious one."[1]

---

1 — Irenaeus, *Against Heresies Book V*, Christian Classics Ethereal Library, accessed April 20, 2023, Ch. 21, https://www.ccel.org/ccel/irenaeus/against_heresies_v.html

What do we believe about Jesus?

We believe in Jesus Christ, the eternal Son of God, incarnated for our redemption, born of the virgin Mary, fully God and fully man, one person in two natures. As our substitute, he lived a sinless life and willingly gave himself as a propitiatory and reconciling sacrifice for our sins on the cross. He died, was buried, rose bodily on the third day, ascended into heaven, and sits at the right hand of God the Father as the only mediator between God and humanity. One day he will return again to judge the living and the dead.

1. Jesus is fully God.

> In the beginning was the Word, and the Word was with God, and the Word was God ... And the Word became flesh and dwelt among us, and we have seen his glory, glory as of the only Son from the Father, full of grace and truth. **JOHN 1:1, 14**

The New Testament declares the full deity of Jesus directly in the above passage and in many others (Colossians 2:9, John 20:28, Hebrews 1:8). The New Testament also declares the full deity of Christ *indirectly* when it reveals Jesus as Creator (Colossians 1:16), Judge (2 Corinthians 5:10), and Savior (Luke 2:11). These are roles only God has. His deity is also confirmed when his followers worshiped him (Matthew 14:33, John 9:38, Luke 24:52). No faithful Jew would ever worship a man unless he believed that man was God.

The early church resisted several heretical teachings that compromised or reduced the divinity of Christ. The church understood that if Jesus were not God, there would be no salvation and no Christianity. They recognized that denying the full deity of Christ was tantamount to renouncing the Christian faith. The result of their defense of the truth was the Nicene Creed (325) and the Chalcedonian Definition (451).

There are several implications of the divinity of Christ.

- Because Jesus is divine, the incarnation is the most important event in history. Everything before it was preparation for the event, and everything after it was the consequence of the event.

- Because Jesus is divine, he could live a sinless life, offer a perfect sacrifice, and bear God's judgment against sin. Only a divine being could pay the price of sin and eradicate our debt.

- Because Jesus is divine, he is all-powerful and can transform our lives.

- Because Jesus is divine, he could conquer death and apply the benefits he earned for us.

- Because Jesus is divine, he has a right to our entire lives. He is the Sovereign Lord, and every knee must bow to him, and every tongue must confess his lordship.

2. Jesus is fully human.

. . . though he was in the form of God, did not count equality with God a thing to be grasped, but emptied himself, by taking the form of a servant, being born in the likeness of men. **PHILIPPIANS 2:6–7**

The eternal Son of God came to earth and took a human nature. Jesus is all God and all man, forever united in one person. We call this the Incarnation. It is closely related to the doctrine of the Trinity. In the Trinity, we learn that Jesus is fully divine, but in the Incarnation, we learn that Jesus is fully man. Together these doctrines capture the two natures of our Savior. These two natures are inseparably united without mixture or loss of separate identity.

Jesus became a man through the Virgin Birth. He was conceived in the womb of Mary by a miraculous work of the Holy Spirit and without a human father. This union guaranteed Christ's true humanity without inherited guilt.

Both natures are necessary for redemption. Christ could represent man and die as a man. All human beings have inherited a corrupt moral nature from their first father, Adam, and are legally guilty before God. If Jesus was not a man, he could not represent fallen humanity.

As God, the death of Christ could have infinite value sufficient to provide redemption for the sins of the world. If Jesus was not God, his death on the cross had no saving power.

Therefore, the Incarnation is an unmistakable reminder that salvation can never come through human effort but must be the work of God himself.

> *In the Trinity, we learn that Jesus is fully divine, but in the Incarnation, we learn that Jesus is fully man.*

3. Jesus is sinless.

For we do not have a high priest who is unable to sympathize with our weaknesses, but one who in every respect has been tempted as we are, yet without sin. **HEBREWS 4:15**

Jesus was a man, but he differed from us in one important way: he was without sin. Because Christ lived a sinless life, his death on the cross was not for his sins but for ours. He met all our salvation needs through his sinless life and sacrificial death.

In order for God to grant us eternal life, we must meet two requirements. We must have a perfect and perpetual record of obedience to God's law, and someone must remove the guilt and penalty of our sin. Christ's sacrificial death meets the second requirement (discussed in the next section), and his sinless life meets the first.

Christ had to live a life of perfect obedience to God to earn righteousness for us. He had to obey the law for his whole life on our behalf so that God would count the merits of his perfect obedience for us. "For as by one man's disobedience many were made sinners, so by one man's obedience many will be made righteous" (Romans 5:19).

Throughout Christ's life, he never sinned; he never yielded to temptation, uttered an unkind word, or acted from selfish motives. His testimony was that he always did the things pleasing to the Father (John 8:29).

Although Jesus did not sin, he waged a lifetime war with the devil. He was tempted in the same way that we are. But he fought the good fight by "offering up prayers and supplications, with loud cries and tears, to him who was able to save him from death," and "he learned obedience through what he suffered" (Hebrew 5:7–8).

His sinlessness is a glaring contrast to the sinfulness of humanity. People without God are hostile to him and cannot submit to his law. Impurity, idolatry, strife, jealousy, anger, envy, evil desire, and greed fill their hearts, and they are desperately sick and dead in sin. That is why Christ's sinlessness identifies him as the divine Son.

He lived a life of perfect obedience as a representative of his people. And now our redemption rests upon his sinless life and substitutionary death.

4. Jesus died for our sins.

> But God shows his love for us in that while we were still sinners, Christ died for us. **ROMANS 5:8**

In our last section, we examined how Christ's sinless life met the requirement of a perfect and perpetual record of obedience to God's law. This section will examine the second requirement: someone must remove the guilt and penalty of our sin.

Christ's death was a substitution. He took our place and bore the penalty of our sin. His substitutionary death provides four salvation needs.

- We deserve to bear God's righteous wrath against sin. "For the wrath of God is revealed from heaven against all ungodliness and unrighteousness of men" (Romans 1:18). Jesus bore the intense hatred of sin that God had patiently stored up since the beginning of the world. At the cross, the fury of that stored-up wrath was unleashed. God the Father inflicted the penalty of sin upon his Son. God the Son voluntarily took upon himself the penalty for sin. Christ's death turned aside God's righteous wrath against sin. "He loved us and sent his Son to be the propitiation for our sins" (1 John 4:10).

- We are separated from God by our sins. "Your iniquities have made a separation between you and your God" (Isaiah 59:2). Christ's death restored us to a relationship with God. "God . . . reconciled us to himself through Christ" (2 Corinthians 5:18–19).

- We are in bondage to sin and the kingdom of Satan. "Everyone who practices sin is a slave to sin" (John 8:34). Christ's death purchased us from the slave market of sin. "In him we have redemption through his blood, the forgiveness of our trespasses" (Ephesians 1:7).

- We are totally depraved and unable to save ourselves. "None is righteous, no, not one; no one seeks for God. No one does good, not even one" (Romans 3:10–12). Christ's death provides us with a new nature if we repent and believe the gospel. "If anyone is in Christ, he is a new creation" (2 Corinthian 5:17).

5. Jesus rose from the dead.

> *For I delivered to you as of first importance what I also received: that Christ died for our sins in accordance with the Scriptures, that he was buried, that he was raised on the third day in accordance with the Scriptures.* **1 CORINTHIANS 15:3, 4**

If Christ was raised from the dead, our faith is secure. If he was not raised from the dead, our faith is in vain, and we are still dead in our sins (1 Corinthians 15:17). As historian Philip Schaff said, "A gospel of a dead Savior would be a contradiction and wretched delusion."[1]

The following three statements are essential results of the resurrection:

Christ's resurrection ensures our salvation.

Peter wrote, "According to his great mercy, he has caused us to be born again to a living hope through the resurrection of Jesus Christ from the dead" (1 Peter 1:3). When Jesus rose from the dead, he earned a new life for us. When we become Christians, we do not receive all of that "resurrection life" because our bodies remain as they are, still subject to weakness, aging, and death. But in our spirits, we are made alive with new resurrection power.

But in our spirits, we are made alive with new resurrection power.

Christ's resurrection ensures that we have power over sin.

The ethical application of the resurrection is the obligation to stop yielding to sin. When Paul says we should consider ourselves "dead to sin and alive to God in Christ Jesus" because of his resurrection power within us (Romans 6:11), he follows immediately with, "Let not sin therefore reign in your mortal bodies.... Do not yield your members to sin" (Romans 6:12-13). Paul uses the fact of our new resurrection power over the domination of sin in our lives as a reason to urge us not to sin anymore.

Christ's resurrection ensures our glorification.

Paul wrote, "... who, by the power that enables him to bring everything under his control, will transform our lowly bodies so that they will be like his glorious body" (Philippians 3:21 NIV). Christ's resurrection was not simply a coming back from the dead. His resurrection was the first fruits of a new kind of human life, a life in which he will make our bodies perfect, no longer subject to weakness, aging, or death, and able to live eternally.

1 — Philip Schaff, *History of the Christian Church, Vol. 1* (Edinburgh: T. & T. Clark, 1893), 172-173.

MEMORY VERSE

In the beginning was the Word, and the Word was with God, and the Word was God ... And the Word became flesh and dwelt among us, and we have seen his glory, glory as of the only Son from the Father, full of grace and truth. **JOHN 1:1, 14**

Application Questions ✎

Which of the five implications of Christ's divinity (page 33) are the most applicable to you currently? Why?

How does Christ's victory free us from bondage, and how do we practically apply it to our lives?

How can we apply Christ's gift of righteousness and his victorious example to our battle against sin?

Meditate on the following passages. What do these passages reveal about Jesus?
Luke 2:1–21; 2:41–52; 3:1–22; 9:28–36; 23:26–43; 24:1–12; 36–49

Discussion Questions

What is at stake if we deny the Virgin Birth?

||||||||||||||||||||||||||||||||||||||||||||||||||||||||||||||||||||||||||||||||||||||||||||

Why is it so difficult to believe that we are totally depraved and unable to save ourselves?

||||||||||||||||||||||||||||||||||||||||||||||||||||||||||||||||||||||||||||||||||||||||||||

Why have skeptics and intellectuals challenged the doctrine of the resurrection so vigorously?

And Can It Be That I Should Gain?

Written by Charles Wesley

And can it be that I should gain
An int'rest in the Savior's blood?
Died He for me, who caused His pain?
For me, who Him to death pursued?
Amazing love! how can it be
That Thou, my God, should die for me?

Refrain:
Amazing love! how can it be
That Thou, my God, should die for me!

'Tis mystery all! Th'Immortal dies!
Who can explore His strange design?
In vain the firstborn seraph tries
To sound the depths of love divine!
'Tis mercy all! let earth adore,
Let angel minds inquire no more. [Refrain]

He left His Father's throne above,
So free, so infinite His grace;
Emptied Himself of all but love,
And bled for Adam's helpless race;
'Tis mercy all, immense and free;
For, O my God, it found out me. [Refrain]

Long my imprisoned spirit lay
Fast bound in sin and nature's night;
Thine eye diffused a quick'ning ray,
I woke, the dungeon flamed with light;
My chains fell off, my heart was free;
I rose, went forth and followed Thee. [Refrain]

No condemnation now I dread;
Jesus, and all in Him is mine!
Alive in Him, my living Head,
And clothed in righteousness divine,
Bold I approach th'eternal throne,
And claim the crown, through Christ my own. [Refrain]

Charles Wesley was born in 1707, the youngest son and nineteenth child of Reverend Samuel and Susanna Wesley. He trained for the ministry at Oxford and, in 1735, was ordained an Anglican minister. He labored with his brother John for nearly fifty years, encouraging and strengthening the Methodist societies throughout Britain.

John's gifts were organizing, writing, and preaching, but Charles was a hymn writer—advancing the Methodist movement through song. Called the "Poet of Methodism," he averaged ten poetic lines a day for fifty years, totaling 8,989 hymns in fifty-six volumes. The most well-known are: "Hark! The Herald Angels Sing," "O for a Thousand Tongues to Sing," "Jesus, Lover of My Soul," and "Christ the Lord Is Risen Today." One historian noted, "The early Methodists were taught and led as much through hymns as through sermons and pamphlets."

Wesley wrote this hymn in 1738 to celebrate his conversion.

YouTube

And Can It Be That I Should Gain

Melharmonic Music Services

CHAPTER 5

The Doctrine of the
Gospel

Merciful and eternal God, heavenly Father, in your tender love towards humanity, you sent your Son, our Savior Jesus Christ, to take on himself flesh and to suffer the bitter death on the cross. We thank you for revealing the glory of your Son and letting the light of your gospel shine on us. In your boundless mercy, help us hold on to this blessed light of your Word, and through your Holy Spirit, govern and guide our hearts so that we may never stray from it, but stand on it and hold fast to it through your Son, Jesus Christ our Lord. For he alone is our righteousness and wisdom, our comfort and peace.[1]

---

1 — Adapted from the sixteenth-century liturgies of the *Book of Common Prayer* and the *Pomeranian Agenda* by Johannes Bugenhagen, a co-laborer with Martin Luther.

The Bible describes the gospel in extraordinary terms. It is the power of God (Romans 1:16). It is the light of the glory of God (2 Corinthians 4:4, 6). It reveals the righteousness of God (Romans 1:17). It is the message that saves us (1 Corinthians 15:1) and blesses the whole world (Galatians 3:8). Through it, we share in the glory of Jesus (2 Thessalonians 2:14). And even the angels long to look into it (1 Peter 1:12).

The gospel is the only way to discover what is wrong with us individually and corporately—every other solution to our problems is incomplete and flawed. But the gospel provides the answer and the power. So, we must preach it to ourselves every day. Martin Luther, commenting on our daily need for the gospel, said, "The Gospel is the principle article of all Christian doctrine. It is necessary that we know this article well, teach it to others, and beat it into their heads continually."

Luther understood what he was talking about through his own experiences. The modern Church owes a considerable debt to him and his gospel teaching.

Martin Luther

When Martin Luther (1483–1546) was twenty-two, a severe lightning storm caught him walking to his home. Thinking he might die, he cried to one of the Roman Catholic saints, "Help me St. Anna, and I will become a monk." When he survived the storm, he entered the Augustinian monastery only to discover that his agonizing attempts to gain assurance of salvation brought him no peace. "For however irreproachably I lived as a monk, I felt myself in the presence of God to be a sinner with a most unquiet conscience. I did not love, indeed I hated this just God, if not with open blasphemy, at least with huge murmuring, for I was indignant against him . . . and yet I continued to knock away at the Apostle Paul, thirsting ardently to know what he really meant."

During this time, he came to believe that Christians are not saved by their efforts but by the gift of God, accepted by faith. "I was seized with the conviction that I must understand Paul's letter to the Romans . . . but the phrase in chapter one stood in my way, 'in it the righteousness of God is revealed.' . . . At last, meditating day and night and by the mercy of God, I began to understand that the righteousness of God is that through which the righteous live by a gift of God, namely by faith . . . Here I felt as if I were entirely born again and had entered paradise itself through gates that had been flung open."

On October 31, 1517, stirred by the Roman Catholic practice of selling indulgences, he nailed his Ninety-five Theses on the cathedral door in Wittenberg, Germany. Within months, copies circulated throughout Europe, drastically reducing the sale of indulgences. This caused a firestorm that the Roman church could not ignore.

When Emperor Charles V summoned him to renounce his teachings at the Diet of Worms in 1521, Luther said, ". . . I am conquered by the Holy Scriptures, and my conscience is bound in the word of God: I cannot and will not recant anything, since it is unsafe and dangerous to do anything against the conscience. Here I stand. I can do no other. God help me!"

Luther's actions and writings ushered in a new era of gospel preaching. He called the gospel doctrine of Sola Fide (Faith Alone) "the summary of all Christian doctrine" and "the article by which the church stands or falls."

Luther Before the Diet of Worms by Anton von Werner (1843–1915)

What do we believe about the gospel?

We believe *the gospel is the good news that God became man in Jesus Christ to reconcile lost people to himself. He lived a perfect, sinless life on our behalf and died on the cross for our sins. He was buried, and on the third day rose from the dead, securing our redemption forever. Having triumphed over Satan and the forces of darkness, he ascended into heaven as Lord of all. Everyone who repents and believes in him receives forgiveness of sins and eternal life.*

1. The gospel is good news.

O foolish Galatians! Who has bewitched you? It was before your eyes that Jesus Christ was publicly portrayed as crucified. Let me ask you only this: Did you receive the Spirit by works of the law or by hearing with faith? Are you so foolish? Having begun by the Spirit, are you now being perfected by the flesh? **GALATIANS 3:1-3**

The Greek word for gospel is *euangelion*. It consists of the prefix *eu* meaning good and the root *angelos* meaning message or messenger. So, the gospel is "good news." First-century Greeks commonly used the word to refer to the news of historical events. It could be news of a military victory, a significant political change, or the joyous birth of a king's son. Any good news was *euangelion*.

The term appears 130 times in the New Testament and is mentioned by eight of the nine New Testament authors. It was a summary word to represent the complete work Jesus did to redeem us. They chose *euangelion* because their message was good news; it was not good advice. Other religions offered good advice; Christianity offered good news. Advice is what you must do, and news is what has already been done. Because the gospel is a past event, it is news, not advice. We follow advice by works; we receive news by faith.

The believers in Galatia had received the good news of the gospel. But gradually that news had deteriorated to advice. They were now attempting to grow in their Christian life by following advice. Paul called this the works of the Law. We could also call it moralism: the view that we are acceptable to God through our attainments. Moralism is an approach to Christianity that focuses on external behavior. It requires obedience to the commands of God without connecting those commands to what God has done for us in Christ. It is the opposite of the gospel.

Dr. Rice Broocks summarized the gospel this way, "The gospel is the good news that God became man in Jesus Christ. He lived the life we should have lived and died the death we should have died—in our place. Three days later, he rose from the dead, proving that he is the Son of God and offering the gift of salvation to those who repent and believe in him."

We must continually battle to ensure we do not follow the path of the Galatians.

2. Repentance is a change of heart and mind in response to God.

Now after John was arrested, Jesus came into Galilee, proclaiming the gospel of God, and saying, "The time is fulfilled, and the kingdom of God is at hand; repent and believe in the gospel." **MARK 1:14–15**

Salvation is like a two-sided coin. On one side is repentance and on the other side is faith. Repentance is turning from sin; faith is turning to God. Neither can occur without the other, and they must occur together for true conversion. It is contrary to the New Testament to speak about saving faith without repentance from sin. In this section, we will examine repentance, and in the next, we will examine faith.

Jesus captures the essence of our response to the kingdom of God with the simple phrase, "repent and believe the gospel." But what does it mean to repent? To answer that question, we must first explain what it's not. Repentance is not an emotion. The author of Hebrews tells us that Esau was emotionally wrought over his sinful decision to sell his birthright, but "he found no chance to repent" (Hebrews 12:16–17). Emotions might accompany repentance (see David's seven penitential Psalms 6, 32, 38, 51, 102, 130, 143), but they are not repentance.

Repentance is a change of mind. The New Testament authors used the Greek word *metanoia* to describe repentance. The term denotes a fundamental transformation of thought and attitude. It is a complete change of orientation that leads to action and new behavior. It is absolute surrender to the will of God that produces a sincere commitment to walk in obedience to Christ and to direct the course of our future according to his plans. It is turning away from anything seeking to usurp Christ's lordship of our lives.

God gives us the gift of repentance (Acts 11:18, 2 Timothy 2:25) by revealing his holiness and our sinfulness (Isaiah 6:3–8). But it is also a decision we make. We make that decision at the point of conversion and every day after that.

Repentance is one of the gospel's load-bearing walls. If we remove it from the gospel, our entire message collapses. Let us diligently hold onto the doctrine of repentance.

3. Faith is believing and trusting in Jesus.

Now Jesus did many other signs in the presence of the disciples, which are not written in this book; but these are written so that you may believe that Jesus is the Christ, the Son of God, and that by believing you may have life in his name. **JOHN 20:30–31**

Saving faith requires that we believe in Jesus and trust in him. To believe in Jesus, we must know the essential facts about his life, death, and resurrection. Belief requires knowledge—we must know God's Word before we can believe it—but it is not enough. Knowledge is a function of the head; believing is a function of the heart. "For with the heart one believes and is justified" (Romans 10:10).

Although knowledge is the starting point of faith, by itself it may just be mental assent—agreeing with the truth of the Bible without personally appropriating it. Mental assent is agreeing with the Word of God in the mind without believing it in the heart. In his sermon, "The Way to the Kingdom," John Wesley said, "Christian faith is not only an assent to the whole gospel of Christ but also a full reliance on the blood of Christ—a resting upon him as our atonement and our life. It is not mental assent to propositions but sure trust and confidence in Christ."

To trust in Jesus, we must be convinced he will do what he said he would. This requires us to surrender our lives to him. We can believe in a set of doctrines, but we must trust in a person. The Apostle John said, "We have come to know and to believe the love that God has for us" (1 John 4:16).

A right definition of faith must include the idea that it is a firm and certain confidence in God's benevolence toward us. This sure knowledge of God's loving character is founded upon the truth of the freely given promise in Christ, both revealed to our minds and sealed upon our hearts through the Holy Spirit.

Let us ensure that our faith in God includes a commitment to the truth and the person of Jesus.

To trust in Jesus, we must be convinced he will do what he said he would.

4. Everyone who repents and believes receives forgiveness.

But what does it say? "The word is near you, in your mouth and in your heart" (that is, the word of faith that we proclaim); because, if you confess with your mouth that Jesus is Lord and believe in your heart that God raised him from the dead, you will be saved. **ROMANS 10:8–9**

We need forgiveness because God is just, and sin makes us guilty and condemned under his righteous judgment. God could not pass over our sins and remain just; we must pay for them. But we cannot pay the debt ourselves because, as Martin Luther said, "Sin is not canceled by man-invented works, for the more a person seeks credit for himself by his own efforts, the deeper he goes into debt."

We are desperate for someone to pay our debt, but who could pay a debt like that? It must be someone who had never sinned and did not owe the debt. This person must be like us so he could take our place but unlike us so that he could pay the infinite price. And so, God the judge became the one who was judged. Our guilt was laid on him. Our death sentence was lifted when the Son of God took our place. His substitutionary death upholds God's justice and allows for our forgiveness. Now we can receive mercy instead of punishment. Charles Wesley summarized this teaching in his hymn, "'Tis Finished, the Messiah Dies":

> Accomplished is the sacrifice
> The great redeeming work is done
> 'Tis finished! All the debt is paid
> Justice divine is satisfied
> The grand and full atonement made
> God for a guilty world has died.

Other religions discuss forgiveness but never on the basis of a divine Savior who pays our debt to a holy God. The Christian doctrine of forgiveness is unique. Marghanita Laski was an English novelist and professed atheist. Shortly before she died in

1988, she said in a television interview, "What I envy most about you Christians is your forgiveness; I have nobody to forgive me."

We cannot receive this forgiveness through labor, zeal, or tears (to paraphrase the hymn, "Rock of Ages"). It only comes when we confess Christ as our Lord (repentance) and believe in our hearts that God raised him from the dead (faith).

5. Everyone who repents and believes receives eternal life.

> And this is the testimony, that God gave us eternal life, and this life is in his Son. Whoever has the Son has life; whoever does not have the Son of God does not have life. **1 JOHN 5:11–12**

Eternal life is a future reward. It is a perpetual and unending life that God gives freely to those who repent and believe. "For the wages of sin is death, but the free gift of God is eternal life in Christ Jesus our Lord" (Romans 6:23). The gift of eternal life contrasts with the death that is the natural result of sin.

The Bible describes this future reward with many images and metaphors. It is a city with mansions and jewels. There are gates of pearl and streets of gold. There is a flowing river and a tree of life. The mountains drip with wine, the hills flow with milk, and all the earth is full of the knowledge of the Lord as the waters cover the sea. And on that day, the Lord will be king over all the earth.

Eternal life is not just a future reward but also a current status. It is a quality of life we experience when we repent and believe. The New Testament word for eternal contains both ideas of duration and quality. The term does not just refer to the future but also to the superior experience of the present age. We do not have to wait for eternal life; it is our current possession. Jesus used the present tense when he said in John 3:36, "Whoever believes in the Son has eternal life." Thus, we live in eternal life right now, experiencing this quality of God's life as a present possession.

The quality of eternal life is best expressed in Jesus' words to his disciples in the upper room: "And this is eternal life, that they know you, the only true God, and Jesus Christ whom you have sent" (John 17:3). This is the heart of eternal life: an authentic and personal relationship with Jesus.

This is the heart of eternal life: an authentic and personal relationship with Jesus

MEMORY VERSE

But what does it say? "The word is near you, in your mouth and in your heart" (that is, the word of faith that we proclaim); because, if you confess with your mouth that Jesus is Lord and believe in your heart that God raised him from the dead, you will be saved. **ROMANS 10:8–9**

Application Questions ✎

The first of Martin Luther's Ninety-five Theses was, "When our Lord and Master Jesus Christ said, 'Repent,' he intended that the entire life of believers should be repentance." What do you think Luther meant by that statement? How does it apply to your life?

Why is mental assent such a danger to believers? How can we be aware of it so we can eliminate it from our lives?

Why is it hard for humans to accept forgiveness? What challenges have you faced in receiving forgiveness, and how have you overcome them?

Pray for an opportunity to share the gospel with someone this week.

Discussion Questions

What is the difference between news and advice, and how does it relate to our Christian life?

|||||||||||||||||||||||||||||||||||||||||||||||||||||||||||||||||||||||||

The Church has tended toward moralism throughout its history. Why is it so appealing, and how can we resist it?

|||||||||||||||||||||||||||||||||||||||||||||||||||||||||||||||||||||||||

It is common in the contemporary church world to exclude the doctrine of repentance from any discussion of salvation. Why do you think that is?

When I Survey the Wondrous Cross

Written by Isaac Watts

When I survey the wondrous cross
On which the Prince of Glory died
My richest gain I count but loss,
And pour contempt on all my pride.

Forbid it, Lord, that I should boast,
Save in the death of Christ my God:
All the vain things that charm me most,
I sacrifice them to his blood.

See from his head, his hands, his feet,
Sorrow and love flow mingled down!
Did e'er such love and sorrow meet?
Or thorns compose so rich a crown?

His dying crimson, like a robe,
Spreads o'er his body on the tree.
Then I am dead to all the globe,
And all the globe is dead to me.

Were the whole realm of nature mine,
That were an offering far too small.
Love so amazing, so divine,
Demands my soul, my life, my all.

Isaac Watts (1674–1748) was a child prodigy who studied Latin at age four, Greek at nine, French at eleven, and Hebrew at thirteen. He was a scholar in many disciplines. He wrote theological treatises; essays on psychology, astronomy, and philosophy; three volumes of sermons; the first children's hymnal; and a textbook on logic that was the standard for generations.

But he is best known for his hymnody. This hymn was a radical departure from the spiritual songs of the day. The early English hymns used only paraphrased biblical texts. This hymn starts with Galatians 6:14 and then departs from Scripture to scriptural ideas. It is one of the first English-language hymns to use the word "I" and to focus directly on personal religious experience. Watts' hymn is an excellent balance of rich theology, scriptural language, and direct personal experience.

Watts designated this hymn as a Communion song and printed it under the heading, "Crucifixion to the World by the Cross of Christ; Galatians 6:14." (Many hymnals omit the fourth verse.)

YouTube

When I Survey
Every Nation Rosebank Worship

CHAPTER 6

The Doctrine of
Salvation

In confidence of your goodness and great mercy, O Lord, I draw near to you, as a sick person to the healer, as one hungry and thirsty to the fountain of life, as a creature to the creator, as a desolate soul to the great comforter. In you is everything I desire. You are my salvation and my redemption, my justification, my hope, and my strength. I believe in you. I hold fast to you, and I am certain you said, "Whoever believes in me will have eternal life." If I am grieved in conscience, your Word still says, "Your sins are forgiven, and you will have eternal life, and I will raise you on the last day." Bring joy, therefore, to the soul of your servant; for to you, O Lord, have I lifted my soul.[1]

---

1 — Adapted from the prayers of Thomas à Kempis and Martin Luther's Collection of Prayers.

Salvation is the sum total of everything God did for us to deliver us from our lost condition in sin and bring us into a right relationship with him. The heart of salvation is the gospel message which includes regeneration, justification, sanctification, and glorification.

Our works could never bring us salvation. We are sinners by our nature and our deeds. We continually break God's laws and fail to attain his moral standards. We are slaves of sin and helpless to correct our condition or to provide for our spiritual needs. Salvation is the work of God's grace; it is received by faith alone. It is the act of God by which he pardons all our sins, accepts us as righteous before his law, and grants us new life by the Holy Spirit.

A. B. Simpson, the founder of the Christian and Missionary Alliance church, summarized salvation with these words, "Tell rebellious men that God is reconciled, justice is satisfied, sin is paid for, the judgment of the guilty is revoked, the condemnation of the sinner canceled, the curse of the Law blotted out, the gates of heaven opened wide, the power of sin conquered, the guilty conscience healed, the broken heart comforted, and the sorrow and misery of the Fall undone."

It was this message that Catherine Booth and her husband William preached.

Catherine Booth

Catherine Booth (1829–1890) was born in the English Midlands to devout Methodist parents. Her mother taught her to read the Scriptures from a young age, and though she had little formal education, Catherine developed a remarkable mind and an ability to write and speak. When she was a teenager, her family moved to London, and Catherine quickly became involved in social reform movements (temperance and women's rights) associated with Methodism.

In her early twenties, she met and fell in love with a like-minded Methodist reformer and itinerant evangelist named William Booth. After they married, Catherine began to travel with William and join him in evangelistic preaching. Female preachers were rare in the nineteenth century. Still, Catherine and William were convinced that there was a biblical basis for female ministry. They believed that the call to preach the gospel was too important to limit their pool of evangelists.

The Booths' pioneering evangelism and compassionate ministry to the poor and outcast in the city of London would eventually result in the founding of the Salvation Army. Their purpose was "to carry the blood of Christ and the fire of the Holy Ghost into every corner of the world." From 1881 to 1885, they launched a remarkable evangelistic campaign that resulted in 250,000 salvations in just four years. One nineteenth-century commentator observed: "Probably during no one hundred years in the history of the world have there been saved so many thieves, gamblers, drunkards, and prostitutes as during the past quarter of a century through the heroic faith and labors of The Salvation Army."

The ministry impact of the Salvation Army was rooted in their conviction that God saves sinful people by grace through faith. Catherine once said, "What the law tried to do by a restraining power from without, the gospel does by an inspiring power from within." The Booths preached this gospel in every corner of London and eventually across the world. Today, the Salvation Army has over 1.2 million "soldiers" (lay ministers) and ministers in 131 nations.

A Sketch of Catherine Booth by Brigadier Mildred Duff.

What do we believe about salvation?

We believe *that salvation, planned in eternity and promised throughout Scripture, is God's gracious act of rescue whereby he delivers lost and sinful people through faith in Christ's redemptive work. Because of his great love, God makes people spiritually alive in Christ through regeneration by the Holy Spirit. By grace, God forgives and justifies people through faith, apart from works, conferring upon them all the benefits of union with Christ, including the gift of God's righteousness, the indwelling Holy Spirit, and adoption into his family.*

1. God planned salvation in eternity.

> *Blessed be the God and Father of our Lord Jesus Christ, who has blessed us in Christ with every spiritual blessing in the heavenly places, even as he chose us in him before the foundation of the world, that we should be holy and blameless before him. In love he predestined us for adoption to himself as sons through Jesus Christ, according to the purpose of his will.* **EPHESIANS 1:3–5**

In his letter to the Ephesians, Paul exalts God for the salvation he gave to those who are in Christ. He wanted all believers to join him in celebrating the greatness of God and the salvation that belongs to us in Jesus. Paul referred to this salvation as the riches of God's glorious inheritance in the saints. God already chose us in Christ before he created the world so that we might be set apart as his children, forgiven and without blame.

Believers differ in understanding Paul's language of God's eternal choice and its relationship to his foreknowledge. But what is certain is that God planned our salvation before we existed. He knew we would need his mercy and deliverance from sin before he created the universe. Paul clearly states that God was motivated by love in planning our salvation. His choice to save us was not made reluctantly or under obligation but by his good pleasure. God loves us, and it pleases him to save us. It is a comfort to know that we were already in God's mind and heart long before we were born.

God wants each of us assured of his great love for us and eternal commitment to fulfill his salvific purpose for us. We should often pray Paul's prayer that the God of our Lord Jesus Christ would give us wisdom and revelation to know him and the hope he has given us. His great power ensures we will receive the riches of his glorious inheritance secured for us by his Son. God has planned a great salvation for everyone who trusts in Jesus Christ.

2. God saves people by grace through faith.

> *For by grace you have been saved through faith. And this is not your own doing; it is the gift of God, not a result of works, so that no one may boast.* **EPHESIANS 2:8–9**

Paul emphasized in all his writings that salvation is God's gracious gift to us who believe; it is not something we earn or achieve through our good works. He consistently taught that we are sinful and that no amount of good works can make up for our sins. There is nothing we can do to become deserving of God's salvation. So, God planned and acted to save us, not because he was obligated to do so, but because of his great love for us. Because of the richness of his mercy, he chose to make us alive in Christ even when we were dead in our sins.

We experience this salvation when we believe the good news that God sent his Son to suffer and die for our sins and rise from the dead to immortal life. God is the one who saves us through his Son, Jesus Christ. We do not save ourselves by earning a righteous standing through good works. This cannot qualify us for God's salvation. Salvation is his gracious gift to us, secured by Jesus and freely given apart from works. As a result, none of us have any grounds to boast about ourselves. We can only boast in Jesus.

Knowing God saves us by grace through faith produces peace in our souls. If we think we must work to earn God's salvation, we will live with constant anxiety, wondering if we have done enough. Or we may succumb to an ugly pride through ignorance of our sinfulness. This pride will make us critical of others we deem to be less holy.

Our hearts can only find rest when we embrace God's gracious gift of salvation in the light of his holiness and our sinfulness.

3. The Holy Spirit regenerates lost, sinful people.

> *But when the goodness and loving kindness of God our Savior appeared, he saved us, not because of works done by us in righteousness, but according to his own mercy, by the washing of regeneration and renewal of the Holy Spirit, whom he poured out on us richly through Jesus Christ our Savior.* **TITUS 3:4–6**

Paul wrote to Titus to instruct him on how to lead the church at Crete. He repeatedly emphasized the need to teach the believers to live godly lives full of good works. Formerly, they were like all humans, sinful and sinning. But God had saved them. The Holy Spirit brought their spiritual rebirth, just as Jesus discussed with Nicodemus (John 3).

This new birth did not happen because they had done anything to deserve it but because God was merciful, kind, and loving. The Holy Spirit renewed them to live a new life of godliness. Therefore, they could renounce sin and live for God as they awaited the return of Jesus Christ.

Elsewhere, Paul adamantly taught that all of us

have sinned and are incapable of fundamentally altering our internal sinful condition. He described us as dead in our sins and enslaved to evil ways. Indeed, all humans are sinners by nature and by choice. Consequently, we are helpless to bring about our spiritual regeneration to be like God in holiness and righteousness. Only God can bring about this change through the Holy Spirit, who imparts God's new life to lost, sinful people. It is his work that causes us to be spiritually regenerated and renewed.

We must never forget that we did not save ourselves. Before we were born of the Spirit, we could not see or enter the kingdom of God. But because we believed in Jesus, God granted us the right to become his children. He caused us to be born again by the Holy Spirit. Therefore, let us pray that God would empower us to boldly communicate the good news of Jesus Christ to others so that others might also experience the Holy Spirit's regenerating work.

4. Believers are united with Christ.

I have been crucified with Christ. It is no longer I who live, but Christ who lives in me. And the life I now live in the flesh I live by faith in the Son of God, who loved me and gave himself for me. **GALATIANS 2:20**

Paul wrote to the Galatian believers to emphasize that the basis for God's salvation was what Jesus had already done. Their faith, not their works, had united them with Christ. He had died for them so that they might live with him and for him. Paul taught that all believers are in Christ, and Christ is in them. They are all one in Christ Jesus, children of God with equal standing. Each of them had received the Spirit of God's Son into their hearts, crying out, "Abba! Father!" Paul wanted to assure them of their union with Christ so that they might learn to live their lives in and through Christ.

Paul repeatedly used the phrase "in Christ" to describe our current spiritual standing and reality as believers. We do not simply believe in a Savior far away from us in heaven, but we are spiritually

On the day when we see him face to face, we will realize the full extent of the bond he has established with us.

joined to him so that he is in us and we are in him. There is no power, person, or presence that can destroy our spiritual union with him. God's great love for us and the work Christ accomplished on our behalf when he died for our sins and rose from the dead is the basis for our bond with Christ.

We must learn to live by faith in Christ, who lives in us. The more we become aware of the reality of our union with him, the more we can learn to rely on him in our daily lives. Though we do not see him now, he is always with us. We are never alone. On the day when we see him face to face, we will realize the full extent of the bond he has established with us. Let us, therefore, grow in our awareness of his presence in our lives now.

5. God credits righteousness to believers.

> *But now the righteousness of God has been manifested apart from the law, although the Law and the Prophets bear witness to it—the righteousness of God through faith in Jesus Christ for all who believe.* **ROMANS 3:21–22**

Paul wrote to the believers in Rome, explaining many central truths concerning God's salvation and how it applied to Jews and non-Jews. Paul taught that all have sinned and cannot achieve God's righteousness. Nevertheless, he has provided the gift of his righteousness to everyone who trusts in Jesus Christ. Jesus himself lived a sinless life, a life of perfect obedience to God. Amazingly, God now credits and imparts Jesus' righteousness to everyone who believes this good news.

In the great exchange, Christ voluntarily took the punishment for our sins upon himself and, in return, gave us his righteousness. When God looks upon us, he sees us clothed with Christ's righteousness. Though we are still not yet what we will be, he already regards us as righteous as Jesus. This is extraordinary. Despite our past sins and our present imperfection, God credits us with the righteousness of his Son. We can boldly walk with God and live for him through the gift of his righteousness and the abundance of his grace.

Because of God's gift of righteousness, we need no longer live under any sense of divine condemnation.

Because of God's gift of righteousness, we need no longer live under any sense of divine condemnation. God is not against us; he is for us. God gave his Son to absorb the punishment of our sin in his own body. Jesus voluntarily died in our place so that we might become the righteousness of God. We must reject every word, thought, and feeling that contradicts God's declaration that we are righteous in Christ. His gift of righteousness has opened the door to unbroken fellowship with him. We can always go to him for help and grace even when we feel unworthy because Jesus' perfect obedience to the Father is the basis of our relationship with him.

MEMORY VERSE

For by grace you have been saved through faith. And this is not your own doing; it is the gift of God, not a result of works, so that no one may boast. **EPHESIANS 2:8–9**

Application Questions ✎

How should the knowledge of being saved by grace through faith affect your life?

How do you think God views you? Why?

Which truths expressed in this section would be most appealing to someone you know who does not yet trust and follow Jesus?

Write your salvation story according to the following framework. It should contain three sections:

- **Pre-conversion:** What lies and sins characterized my old life, and what were their consequences?
- **Conversion:** What truths and events brought me to the point of salvation, and how did I respond?
- **Post-conversion:** How did God's love and lordship change my life, and how is it continuously changing me?"

Tell your salvation story to one person this week.

Discussion Questions

Why is it significant that God planned our salvation before he even created the universe?

|||||||||||||||||||||||||||||||||||||||||||||||||||||||||||||||||||||||||||

What does it mean to say we are saved by grace through faith?

|||||||||||||||||||||||||||||||||||||||||||||||||||||||||||||||||||||||||||

What are some implications of being adopted into God's family and given the gift of God's righteousness?

Rock of Ages

Written by Augustus Montague Toplady

Rock of Ages, cleft for me,
let me hide myself in thee;
let the water and the blood,
from thy wounded side which flowed,
be of sin the double cure;
save from wrath and make me pure.

Not the labors of my hands
can fulfill thy law's demands;
could my zeal no respite know,
could my tears forever flow,
all for sin could not atone;
thou must save, and thou alone.

Nothing in my hand I bring,
simply to the cross I cling;
naked, come to thee for dress;
helpless, look to thee for grace;
foul, I to the fountain fly;
wash me, Savior, or I die.

While I draw this fleeting breath,
when mine eyes shall close in death,
when I soar to worlds unknown,
see thee on thy judgment throne,
Rock of Ages, cleft for me,
let me hide myself in thee.

Augustus Montague Toplady (1740–1778) was born to Irish parents in a village outside of London. His father died when he was young, and his mother enrolled him in the prestigious Westminster School. After graduation, he moved to Ireland to attend Trinity College, Dublin. In his sixteenth year, he attended a gospel meeting where he confessed Christ. He said of the experience, "Strange that I who had so long sat under the means of grace in England should be brought right unto God in an obscure part of Ireland, amidst a handful of people met together in a barn, and by the ministry of one who could hardly spell his own name. Surely it was the Lord's doing, and it is marvelous."

His hymn has comforted men and women everywhere since it was first published. When the British steamship the SS London sank in the Bay of Biscay in 1866 and 220 people died, the last thing heard by the nineteen survivors was the voices of the doomed passengers singing "Rock of Ages."

YouTube

Rock of Ages Cleft for Me
Jehovah Shalom Acapella

CHAPTER 7

The Doctrine of the
Holy Spirit

Father in heaven, you sent your Son to reveal yourself to us, your Father-love, and all that love has for us. And he has taught us that the Holy Spirit is the gift above all gifts you would bestow in answer to prayer.

O, my Father. I come to you with this prayer; there is nothing I desire so much as to be filled with the Holy Spirit. The blessings he brings are unspeakable and just what I need. He sheds abroad your love in my heart. I long for this. He breathes the mind and life of Christ in me so that I live as he did, in and for the Father's love. I long for this. He endues with power from on high for all my walk and work. I long for this. O, Father, I ask you, give me this day the fulness of your Spirit.

Father! I ask this, resting on the words of my Lord: "How much more the Holy Spirit." I believe you hear my prayer; I receive now what I ask, Father! I claim, and I take it, the fulness of the Spirit as mine. I welcome the gift this day again as a faith gift; in faith, I reckon my Father works through the Spirit all he has promised. Amen.[1]

---

1 — Adapted from Andrew Murray, *With Christ in the School of Prayer.*

For nearly three years, Jesus trained his disciples to bring the message of repentance and faith to the world. Yet before he left, he commanded them to wait until they had received the Father's promised Holy Spirit and were clothed with power. Once the Holy Spirit came upon them at Pentecost, they were then to go to their city, region, and all the nations as his witnesses.

As the Holy Spirit was intimately involved in the Church's missionary activity from the beginning, he still is—energizing us to do the work of the ministry. God desires to manifest his power among the nations, and this manifestation comes from the Holy Spirit. The Spirit works miracles and healings and reveals revelational knowledge, wisdom, and prophecies through us for his glory.

Without the Holy Spirit's help, we can engage in religious activity but fail to advance his kingdom. But we can do everything God has called us to do with the Holy Spirit's power. God wants to repeatedly fill each of us with his Spirit, empowering us for his service. He urges us to earnestly desire the Spirit's empowerment to serve others and draw them to Christ.

At the outset of the twentieth century, God poured out the Holy Spirit in miraculous demonstrations in several places worldwide. One of them was Los Angeles, and the instrument was William Seymour.

William Seymour

In 1905, William Seymour (1870-1922), a one-eyed Holiness preacher and the son of former slaves, heard Charles Parham teach on the Baptism in the Holy Spirit in Houston, Texas. Parham would not allow Seymour in the classroom, so he sat in the hall and received the Pentecostal doctrine.

When Seymour was filled with the Holy Spirit he said: "I could feel the power going through me like electric needles. I was laid out under the power five times before Pentecost came. I talked and laughed with joy far into the night. I received the baptism with the Holy Ghost and fire, and I felt the presence of God in my heart, my hands, my arms, and all through my body."

In February of 1906, he received an invitation to pastor a small Holiness church in Los Angeles. His first sermon in his new church was on the Baptism in the Holy Spirit. When he returned for the evening service, the deacons had padlocked the church to keep him out.

However, a few members followed Seymour and began a Bible study in their home. On April 9, God baptized several of them in the Holy Spirit. Soon the crowds were so great that they could no longer meet in the house. They rented an abandoned church at 312 Azusa Street and held meetings three times a day.

By the summer of 1906, crowds had reached staggering numbers. People flocked from all over the world, and the scene was an international gathering. Every day, trains unloaded visitors from all over the continent. News accounts of the meetings spread in both the secular and religious press. They said of Seymour, "he was not a gifted speaker, he lacked in social skills, and he had almost no formal education."

But God filled him with power and used him to usher in the century of the Holy Spirit. Church historian Vinson Synan has estimated that over 850,000,000 people received the Baptism in the Holy Spirit in the twentieth century.

A picture of William Seymour from the early 1910s.

The Azusa Street church in 1907.

What do we believe about the Holy Spirit?

We believe *in God the Holy Spirit, giver and renewer of life, sent to guarantee our promised future. The Spirit convicts concerning sin, enlightens to the truth, awakens to repentance and faith, regenerates sinners, and unites believers to Christ, making them partakers of the divine nature. By the Spirit's indwelling, Christians enjoy God's presence and fellowship. By being filled with the Holy Spirit, Christians are divinely empowered for witness and ministry. As they bear the fruit of the Spirit and exercise spiritual gifts, believers edify the Church and bear witness to God's kingdom.*

1. The Holy Spirit is fully God.

The grace of the Lord Jesus Christ and the love of God and the fellowship of the Holy Spirit be with you all. **2 CORINTHIANS 13:14**

Paul repeatedly wrote about the Holy Spirit in his letters to the Corinthians. He ascribed divine attributes to him, pointing to the Spirit's coequality with the Father and the Son. In the verse above, Paul blessed the Corinthians with a prayerful benediction, affirming the personhood of Jesus, the Father (whom he customarily referred to as God), and the Holy Spirit. This indicated that the believers in Corinth (and believers everywhere) could know and experience each person of the Triune God. Paul wanted them to enjoy "fellowship" with the Holy Spirit, which meant a close relationship.

The Holy Spirit is described in Scripture as eternal, all-powerful, all-knowing, and everywhere present, just as the Father and the Son are. The biblical authors call him the Spirit of God, the Spirit of the Father, the Spirit of God's Son, the Spirit of Jesus, and the Spirit of Christ. This reveals his essential union with the Father and the Son. His numerous titles, such as the Spirit of truth, the Spirit of holiness, the Spirit of life, the Spirit of grace, and the Spirit of glory, also affirm his divine identity. When Jesus called him "another helper" like himself who would be with the disciples and aid them as Jesus had, he ascribed divine honor to the Holy Spirit. When various authors revealed the Spirit's role in bringing forth and sustaining the creation, they declared that he is fully divine in every way.

The Holy Spirit is not an impersonal force or power. He is a divine person, just as the Father and the Son are divine persons, and we should honor him in that way. We should respond to the invitation to grow in our relationship with each person of the Trinity and genuinely experience Jesus' grace, the Father's love, and the Spirit's fellowship.

2. The Holy Spirit dwells in all believers.

> *And it is God who establishes us with you in Christ, and has anointed us, and who has also put his seal on us and given us his Spirit in our hearts as a guarantee.* **2 CORINTHIANS 1:21–22**

The context of this passage is Paul's affirmation that the Father has made all his promises available to those who trust in Jesus. And the guarantee of those promises was the "seal" of the indwelling Holy Spirit.

Using "seals" in ancient times was a common practice to indicate ownership and completion. The seals were often made of wax and stamped by the personal imprint of their guarantor. All the believers in Corinth would have understood Paul's practice.

Paul's metaphor has two meanings. First, it highlights that we are God's possession. He has put his imprint on us and claimed us as his own family. The Holy Spirit now assures us that we are God's children and stirs our longing to draw near him. He produces the cry, "Abba, Father," within us.

Second, it highlights that the Father will complete what he began in us. An ancient merchant would open one sack of grain and weigh the contents for the buyer. He would then seal the grain sack, pledging that all the other sacks contained the full weight. This metaphor means that the Spirit's continual presence within us reminds us that God will bring about the fullness of our salvation. We will surely inherit everything God had planned and promised.

What a wonderful gift God has given us in the Holy Spirit! We are not only forgiven and reconciled to a distant Father, but God has come to us in the person of his Spirit. We are never alone; he dwells in us and will be with us forever. Christ has secured our union with God, and the Holy Spirit has sealed it. Whatever we may face in our journey through this present life, we can take comfort in knowing God's Spirit is in us and with us. If we turn our hearts and minds toward him, we will find him willing and able to guide us through all life's challenges.

3. The Holy Spirit works salvation in those being saved.

> *Now the Lord is the Spirit, and where the Spirit of the Lord is, there is freedom. And we all, with unveiled face, beholding the glory of the Lord, are being transformed into the same image from one degree of glory to another. For this comes from the Lord who is the Spirit.* **2 CORINTHIANS 3:17–18**

In this part of Paul's second letter to the Corinthians, he compares the glory of the old covenant with the greater glory of the new covenant. He uses the veil that Moses covered his face with as a metaphor for the transforming power of the presence of God.

Under the old covenant, God's glory transformed Moses' outer man and caused his face to shine. Because of this, he needed a veil to protect Israel from the intense light. But in the new covenant, the veil has lifted, and God's glory now transforms our inner man, causing us to reflect his character. And the executor of this transformation is the Holy Spirit. The Holy Spirit liberates us and progressively transforms us into the image of Christ. Though the ministry of God's law was necessary and good for Israel, the ministry of God's Spirit far surpasses it in glory for the Church. For the Spirit can do what the law never could: write God's truth on our hearts.

The Holy Spirit is involved in every aspect of our salvation, from our initial conversion to our final glorification. Only with his ongoing work can we grow in salvation. He works in us the desire to obey God and imparts the ability to do so. He imparts God's life to us, reveals truth to us, guides us, comforts us, encourages us, and emboldens us. Without him, we are spiritually helpless.

We must take to heart Paul's admonition to the Galatian believers (Galatians 3:1-6). He chastised them for resorting to self-reliance after initially believing in Christ and receiving the Holy Spirit. Instead, we must trust in Jesus and rely on the Holy Spirit for every aspect of our spiritual lives and growth. Doing so will ensure our humility and reception of God's endless mercy and grace to help us in every need. Let us, therefore, make every effort to cooperate with him.

4. The Holy Spirit manifests God's presence and power.

Now there are varieties of gifts, but the same Spirit; and there are varieties of service, but the same Lord; and there are varieties of activities, but it is the same God who empowers them all in everyone. To each is given the manifestation of the Spirit for the common good. **1 CORINTHIANS 12:4–7**

The gospel had come to the Corinthians through Paul's preaching, accompanied by the Holy Spirit's presence and power. The Spirit was working miracles and healings among them and revealing revelational knowledge, wisdom, and prophecies. Paul urged the Corinthian believers to yearn for this to continue but not for selfish or pseudo-spiritual reasons. The Spirit's goal in manifesting his presence and power was to draw them to Christ. Even though the Corinthian church was riddled with problems and sins: divisions, drunkenness, lawsuits, immorality, compromise with the culture, disrespect toward leadership, and more, God continued to grace them with spiritual gifts.

Spiritual gifts are manifestations and ministries of the Holy Spirit given to every believer for edification and evangelism until the return of Christ.

> *God desires to manifest his presence and power among us.*

The word gifts in the original language of the New Testament is the same word translated as grace. So, the gifts are works of God's grace in and through the believer. They are outpourings of God's grace manifested in various ways that reveal God's power and love.

God desires to manifest his presence and power among us. He responds to our faith and spiritual hunger, visiting us though we are as imperfect as the Corinthians. We are not qualified to participate in the Spirit's manifestation in our midst, but Jesus is. In him, we may boldly come before God and call upon him to receive his presence and gifts. God does not want us to be satisfied with a non-experiential relationship with him. Christ died and rose again so that God's presence through the Holy Spirit might dwell among us. Let us enjoy his presence.

5. The Holy Spirit empowers believers for service.

But you will receive power when the Holy Spirit has come upon you, and you will be my witnesses in Jerusalem and in all Judea and Samaria, and to the end of the earth. **ACTS 1:8**

Jesus trained his disciples to bring his message of repentance and faith to the world. They were to carry out his mission of reconciliation with God. Yet he told them not to go until they had received the Father's promise of the Holy Spirit, who would clothe them with power. Once the Holy Spirit had come upon them, they were to go to their city, their region, and all the nations as Jesus' witnesses, telling others what Jesus had done and taught.

On the day God first filled Jesus' disciples with the Holy Spirit, Peter preached that God was pouring his Spirit upon all his people: men and women, young and old. The gift of the Spirit's empowering presence is for everyone who repents and believes in Jesus. God excludes no one who comes to him. Joel had prophesied that God would make all of his people prophetic when the Spirit comes upon them. God wants all his children to "hear" the voice of the Holy Spirit, be led by the Spirit, and serve others in words and deeds empowered by the Spirit.

> *We can do everything God has called us to do with the Holy Spirit's help.*

We can do everything God has called us to do with the Holy Spirit's help. Without his help, we can engage in religious activity but fail to advance God's kingdom. God wants to repeatedly fill each of us with his Spirit, empowering and emboldening us for his service. God's Spirit works healings and miracles through us. He reveals knowledge, wisdom, and prophecies through us. God urges us to earnestly desire the Spirit's empowerment to serve others and draw them to Christ. We should keep seeking God and remain hungry and thirsty for his empowering presence.

MEMORY VERSE

"But you will receive power when the Holy Spirit has come upon you, and you will be my witnesses in Jerusalem and in all Judea and Samaria, and to the end of the earth."
ACTS 1:8

Application Questions ✎

In what ways are you aware of the Holy Spirit's involvement in your life?

How can you better honor the Holy Spirit in your life?

Is there anything the Holy Spirit has been addressing in your life that requires your greater attention?

Take fifteen minutes each day this week to record what the Holy Spirit was saying and doing in your life.

Discussion Questions

Why is it important to fully embrace the Holy Spirit as a person and not a divine force or power?

How does the Holy Spirit actualize or make the salvation Jesus procured for us effective?

How does the Holy Spirit empower us for God's service?

Wa Emimimo

NIGERIAN:

Wa wa wa Emimimo. (Emioloye.)
Wa wa wa Alagbaram. (Alagbarameta.)
Wao, wao, wao. (Emimimo.)

ENGLISH:

Come, O Holy Spirit, come. (Holy Spirit, come.)
Come, Almighty Spirit, come. (Almighty Spirit, come.)
Come, come, come. (O Spirit, come.)

Portuguese Catholic missionaries first brought the gospel to West Africa late in the fifteenth century. They introduced worship that was primarily monophonic (single melody) Gregorian chant. When the Protestant missionaries arrived in the middle of the nineteenth century, they brought with them the long tradition of Western hymnody. But it wasn't until the middle of the twentieth century that West African nations began to create their own hymns in their native languages with traditional African musical techniques. These techniques included complex percussive cross-rhythms, congregational clapping using various patterns simultaneously, dancing and processionals, and simple lyrics with repetition.

This song is a good example of some of these characteristics.

YouTube
Emi Mimo (Live)
Omoniyi Oni

CHAPTER 8

The Doctrine of
Missions

We are no longer our own, Lord; we belong to you. So send us wherever you want. Give us the nations for our inheritance and the ends of the earth for our possession. Let our life be a beacon of hope for those whose lives have been devastated by violence, suffering, and loss. Empower us with supernatural wisdom to engage in any situation. Give us the ministry of reconciliation so we may be a bridge to the lost. Fan into flame the global Church so its heart would beat vigorously for the Great Commission. Use us in our homes, workplaces, ministries, and nations so that Jesus would be glorified and your kingdom come to this earth.[1]

---

1 — Adapted from the Lausanne Covenant, John Wesley's Covenant Prayer, and other sources.

The Bible is not a random collection of writings but a single story—a unified record that communicates a coherent and constant message. It is the unfolding drama of God's mission to save a remnant for himself from lost humanity and to shape a new creation from a broken world.

"The Bible presents itself to us fundamentally as a narrative, a historical narrative at one level, but a grand metanarrative at another. It begins with the God of purpose in creation, moves on to the conflict and problem generated by human rebellion against that purpose, spends most of its narrative journey in the story of God's redemptive purposes being worked out on the stage of human history, and finishes beyond the horizon of its own history with the eschatological hope of a new creation."[1]

Missions, then, is not just for missionaries; it is the totality of life. We all are honored to participate in God's mission.

But God has called some men and women throughout history to take his mission to other places and other peoples. Francis Asbury was one of those missionaries.

Francis Asbury

On August 7, 1771, the twenty-six-year-old Francis Asbury (1745–1816) responded to a sermon by John Wesley to go as a missionary to America. Wesley said, "Our brethren in America call aloud for help. Who are willing to go over and help them?"

Asbury was. When he set sail for America, his devout Methodist father wept openly, fearing he would never see his son again. His insight proved to be prophetic.

During the voyage, Asbury recorded in his journal why he was going to America: "I am going to live to God, and to bring others so to do." When he arrived in America, there were four Methodist ministers and about 300 Methodists. Forty-five years later, there were over 2,000 ministers and 214,000 Methodists.

During those forty-five years, he rode more than a quarter million miles on horseback and crossed the Allegheny Mountains sixty times. He visited nearly every state once a year, ordained over 4,000 ministers, and preached at least 17,000 sermons.

Asbury was the only English preacher to support the American cause in the War of Independence. Although every other preacher left for England, he stood, determined to stand or fall with the cause of independence.

His constant travels put a terrible strain on his health, but he labored on despite the cost. He described in his journal a typical winter trip:

> The water froze as it ran from the horse's nostrils. I have suffered a little by lodging in open houses in this cold weather, but this is a very small thing when compared to what the dear Redeemer suffered for the salvation of precious souls.

He died at seventy-one, still attempting to mount his horse for another circuit ride. The passion of his life is evident in one of his journal entries, "My consolations are great. I live in God from moment to moment."

Francis Asbury,
August 1745–
March 31, 1816

---

1 — Christopher Wright, *The Mission of God: Unlocking the Bible's Grand Narrative* (InterVarsity Press, 2006), 63–64.

What do we believe about missions?

We believe *God's mission is to redeem a people for himself from every tribe, nation, and language and to restore creation for his glory. As the Father loved the world and sent his Son, and the Father and the Son sent the Spirit, the Triune God sends the Church into the world to proclaim the gospel, make disciples, and seek God's justice and reconciliation in the world.*

1. God's mission is to redeem a people for himself.

> *After this I looked, and behold, a great multitude that no one could number, from every nation, from all tribes and peoples and languages, standing before the throne and before the Lamb, clothed in white robes, with palm branches in their hands, and crying out with a loud voice, "Salvation belongs to our God who sits on the throne, and to the Lamb!"* **REVELATION 7:9–10**

Ever since Adam and Eve's fall in the Garden of Eden (Genesis 3), God has been on a mission to redeem humanity and all of the created order. God's redemptive mission is not the attempt of a divine watchmaker to fix a broken creation; it is the work of a loving father to restore a broken relationship with his creatures. God has always manifested his redemptive work in the world in particular times and places and with particular people—but always with universal implications.

One early example of God's rescue mission was when he saved Noah's family from the great flood (Genesis 7). His mission continued when he called out Abraham with the promise that he would become a great nation and that God would bless all the nations of the earth through him (Genesis 12). Abraham's descendants became the nation of Israel—God's chosen people. In their unique history chronicled in the Old Testament, God chose and revealed himself to them.

The Israelites were God's chosen people, but he chose them to be a light to all the nations of the earth. This promise was ultimately fulfilled in Jesus—the second person of the Trinity who came into the world as a Jew in the royal line of King David. Jesus focused his brief earthly ministry demonstrating to the Jewish people that he was the Messiah, but his final words made it clear that his disciples should proclaim the good news of his death and resurrection to the ends of the earth. Since then, the Father, through the Son, is still redeeming a people for himself from every tribe, tongue, and nation. This redeemed people from all times, places, and ethnicities is called the Church.

2. God sent his Son and his Spirit to redeem sinful humans.

For God so loved the world, that he gave his only Son, that whoever believes in him should not perish but have eternal life. For God did not send his Son into the world to condemn the world, but in order that the world might be saved through him. **JOHN 3:16-17**

The Bible uses different metaphors to describe the saving work of Jesus—the focal point of God's mission. One of the most common is redemption. The modern world thinks of redemption primarily as a "religious" concept, but the ancient world thought of it in economic terms. To them, it signified the price paid to rescue a slave or prisoner of war. Sometimes the payment was in money (gold, silver, etc.); sometimes the payment was in people (a prisoner exchange). In this passage (and elsewhere in the New Testament, e.g., Mark 10:45), John uses the metaphor to explain why God sent his Son to earth.

The Bible likens our sinful human condition to slavery or captivity to emphasize that we cannot redeem ourselves. This is why Jesus came, to pay the ransom price. But Jesus was not only the broker of our redemption—the person who coordinated the payment—he was the payment itself. Jesus was free, but he gave his life to redeem humans in bondage. He was perfectly holy, but he gave his life for sinful humanity. It was his life for our life.

When Jesus explained this to an inquiring religious leader named Nicodemus, he started with God's motivation in sending him to redeem the world—love. God's redemptive mission flows from his love for sinful humanity. Because he loved the world, he sent Jesus to redeem sinful humans. It is crucial to highlight God's stated motive here because it is also our motive in joining God on mission. God did not redeem us because he needed us or because he was under an obligation to us. God sent his Son to redeem us because he loved us.

3. God sends the Church to proclaim the gospel.

Jesus said to them again, "Peace be with you. As the Father has sent me, even so I am sending you." And when he had said this, he breathed on them and said to them, "Receive the Holy Spirit." **JOHN 20:21–22**

Before Jesus ascended into heaven, he charged his small group of disciples to proclaim the good news of his life, death, and resurrection to the ends of the earth. Jesus used the metaphor of a witness—someone who testifies of what they've seen or heard in a court of law. Whether we are actively proclaiming the good news of the gospel or answering questions about what we've seen or heard about Jesus, the goal is to call all people to repent and believe in the gospel. The first disciples did this with great zeal and courage, which is what every subsequent generation of Christians has tried to do (with greater or less success) for the last two thousand years.

Effective gospel proclamation is only possible when we recognize who is involved. First, it's important to note that this is the Church's calling. Sometimes we can feel overwhelmed by the task and feel like everything is up to us as individual Christians. However, knowing God has called and sent the Church to do this massive work is freeing. It is a multi-ethnic, multi-generational team with different gifts, strengths, and social connections. And it is only as the whole Church that we will effectively proclaim the gospel to the ends of the earth.

As the body of Christ, we are called to continue God's redemptive mission in the earth. As the Father sent the Son to redeem the world, so he sends us—the Church—into the world to bring that good news of his redemption to all people. It is important to remember that when God sent the Church into the world to be his witnesses, he did not send them alone. He sent his Holy Spirit to empower them to be his witnesses. When we preach the gospel, we are not alone. We are on a mission with the whole Church, and the Holy Spirit empowers us.

4. God sends the Church to make disciples.

And Jesus came and said to them, "All authority in heaven and on earth has been given to me. Go therefore and make disciples of all nations, baptizing them in the name of the Father and of the Son and of the Holy Spirit, teaching them to observe all that I have commanded you. And behold, I am with you always, to the end of the age." **MATTHEW 28:18–20**

Gospel proclamation is crucial and primary, but our mission does not stop with preaching or even conversion. Jesus commissioned us to make disciples. Disciples are people who follow Jesus, fellowship with other believers, and fish for people (Matthew 4:19). So we must preach the gospel to make disciples and also teach people to follow Jesus. Conversion is a one-time event when people surrender their lives to Jesus, but discipleship is a lifelong process of following Jesus, becoming more like him, and bringing others on the journey.

We cannot underestimate this call for all followers of Jesus not only to be disciples but to make disciples. So often, people assume that making disciples is the role of professionals (like pastors or campus missionaries), but Jesus made no such distinction. Following him in a discipleship relationship implicates us (the Church) in his mission

of bringing lost people into a relationship with the Father. We are all called to be disciples and disciple-makers. We all have unique spheres of influence. We know people who will only hear the gospel if we share it with them and will only start on the road of discipleship if we walk alongside them.

There are many things to learn in our discipleship journey and many things to pass on to others, but Jesus highlighted one foundational principle that undergirds everything else—obedience. As disciples, we are on a journey of obedience—daily learning how to die to ourselves and submit our lives to the lordship of Jesus. And as disciple-makers, this is what we must teach and encourage others to do. This is hard work, but we must never forget that as we go and make disciples of all nations, Jesus is "with us always to the end of the age."

5. God sends the Church to be a prophetic voice to a sinful world.

> *The Spirit of the Lord is upon me, because he has anointed me to proclaim good news to the poor. He has sent me to proclaim liberty to the captives and recovering of sight to the blind, to set at liberty those who are oppressed, to proclaim the year of the Lord's favor.* **LUKE 4:18–19**

Jesus began his ministry by reading Isaiah 61 aloud to the synagogue in his hometown of Nazareth. After reading this ancient messianic prophecy, he said, "Today this Scripture is fulfilled in your hearing." At that moment, Jesus claimed he was the fulfillment of the prophecy. Profound concern for human suffering would mark his ministry and result in transformative liberation. He would bring healing and freedom to the poor, the brokenhearted, the captives, the blind, and the oppressed. In other words, Jesus' mission—and by extension, his Church's mission—had an other-world and a this-world orientation.

Jesus called his Church to preach the gospel and make disciples. He also called her to heal broken bodies and liberate people from unjust systems. Jesus set the example by preaching to multitudes, healing the sick, and liberating the oppressed. As a consequence, historically, Christians have spearheaded the most significant abolition movements over the last two thousand years and have been at the forefront of providing health care to those who need it most.

> *We must accept that our work will always be incomplete and unfinished.*

It is the work of the Church to seek God's justice and reconciliation in the world as "far as the curse is found" (to quote Isaac Watts in "Joy to the World"). To be a prophetic voice is to see the world's injustice and join with the prophets of old in decrying the oppression of humans made in God's image. To be a prophetic voice is to engage the world with a kingdom-inspired imagination and a Christ-centered hope—to work to see God's kingdom come on earth as it is in heaven. However, we must remember Jesus called us to be prophets, not saviors. We must accept that our work will always be incomplete and unfinished. Only Jesus can finish this work when he returns. Our role is to bear witness to it in small (and occasionally big) ways. We are not the savior of the world—Jesus is.

MEMORY VERSE

And Jesus came and said to them, "All authority in heaven and on earth has been given to me. Go therefore and make disciples of all nations, baptizing them in the name of the Father and of the Son and of the Holy Spirit, teaching them to observe all that I have commanded you. And behold, I am with you always, to the end of the age."
MATTHEW 28:18–20

Application Questions ✎

God's motive for redemption was love: "For God so loved the world, that he gave..." This provides us with the model of what our motive should be in advancing the mission of God. In light of that, what are some hindrances that affect your personal commitment to the mission, and what can you do to resolve them?

As ministers of reconciliation, we all are called to go, pray, and give. Which one is the Holy Spirit emphasizing to you now, and what will you do about it?

Profound concern for human suffering marked Jesus' ministry and resulted in transformative liberation. Consequently, justice and reconciliation should characterize our participation in God's mission. What aspect of this part of God's mission is the Holy Spirit calling you to engage in at a deeper level?

Fast one day for a particular nation or people group.

Discussion Questions

Why is it essential to recognize that God's redemptive work in the world has always manifested itself in particular times, places, and people but with universal implications?

||||||||||||||||||||||||||||||||||||||||||||||||||||||||||||||||||||||||||||||||

Why is discipleship an essential part of our mission? What would our mission look like without discipleship?

||||||||||||||||||||||||||||||||||||||||||||||||||||||||||||||||||||||||||||||||

What are the implications of Jesus' self-declaration in Luke 4:18–19, and how does it apply to the mission of the Church?

Send the Light

Written by Charles Hutchinson Gabriel

There's a call comes ringing o'er the restless wave,
"Send the light! Send the light!"
There are souls to rescue, there are souls to save,
Send the light!
Send the light!

Chorus:
Send the light, the blessed gospel light;
Let it shine from shore to shore!
Send the light the blessed gospel light;
Let it shine forevermore!

We have heard the Macedonian call today,
"Send the light! Send the light!"
And a golden offering at the cross we lay,
Send the light!
Send the light!

Let us pray that grace may ev'rywhere abound,
"Send the light! Send the light!"
And a Christ-like spirit ev'rywhere be found,
Send the light!
Send the light!

Let us not grow weary in the work of love,
"Send the light! Send the light!"
Let us gather jewels for a crown above,
Send the light!
Send the light!

Charles Hutchinson Gabriel (1856–1932) grew up on a farm in the American Midwest. He had no formal musical training but had a gift for singing and composing. He wrote or composed over 7,000 songs using several different pseudonyms. The musical director for the Billy Sunday crusades, Homer Rodeheaver, promoted his songs in their revival meetings and made them popular with the masses. His most well-known hymns are "Will the Circle Be Unbroken" and "His Eye Is on the Sparrow."

YouTube
Send the Light
Lifeway Worship

The Doctrine of the
Church

O God of our salvation, hope of all the ends of the earth, hear us. In your strength, may your Church, as it extends to all corners of the world, soar in faith, rest in hope, and rise to the full height of love. Fill it with all truth. Where it is in error, direct it. Where it is right, strengthen and confirm it. Where it is divided, make it unified. Deliver it from all evil, make it perfect in your love, and sanctify it for the kingdom which you have prepared for it.[1]

---

1 — Adapted from the Mozarabic Liturgy of the Middle Ages, William Laud, and the Didache.

A 2019 survey by LifeWay discovered that sixty-five percent of American churchgoers agree with the statement, "I can walk with God without other believers." This view seems to be prevalent in other parts of the world as well. In contrast to this view, the Bible teaches that the Church is essential for believers.

The Church is the place where believers corporately worship God. It is the base where the world is evangelized and believers are discipled. It is the locus of Christ's continuing activity and the pillar and support of the truth.

Much of what we know and believe about the Church is the product of Augustine of Hippo, one of the most prodigious theologians in history.

Augustine

Augustine (354–430) was born in North Africa to a pagan father and a Christian mother. He followed his mother's faith at an early age, but by sixteen, his pagan education and many passions led him to break with Christianity.

For seventeen years, he experienced periods of immorality, entanglement in appealing philosophies, and spiritual crises. During that time, he taught rhetoric and public speaking in Carthage, Rome, and Milan. In Milan, he came under the influence of Bishop Ambrose and committed his life to Christ. He said about that moment:

> I cast myself down under a fig tree, giving full vent to my tears. I said, "O Lord, how long? Will You be angry forever? Why is there not this hour an end to my uncleanness?" While I was speaking, I heard from a neighboring house a voice of a child chanting, "Take up and read." I arose, interpreting it to be a command from God to open the Bible and read the first chapter I found. It was Romans 13:13–14, "Let us behave decently, as in the daytime, not in orgies and drunkenness, not in sexual immorality and debauchery, not in dissension and jealousy. Rather, clothe yourselves with the Lord Jesus Christ, and do not think about how to gratify the desires of the sinful nature." At the end of this sentence all the darkness of doubt instantly vanished away.

From that moment, he was a changed man, and he devoted his heart and soul to the service of the Church. In 395, he was elected bishop of Hippo against his will, laboring there for thirty-five years until his death. In public debate and through his writings, Augustine defended the teachings of the Church against heretics and schismatics. He molded the theology of the Middle Ages in Europe and greatly influenced Luther and Calvin. Next to the Apostle Paul, he did more to shape Christianity than any other person.

The earliest known portrait of Saint Augustine in a sixth-century fresco, Lateran, Rome.

What do we believe about the Church?

We believe in one holy, universal, and apostolic Church, the body of Christ of which Jesus is the head. As God's holy people on mission, the visible Church is expressed in gathered communities where believers assemble to pray, worship, hear God's Word, receive the sacraments, and fellowship with one another. Through the ministry of his Spirit, faithful disciples, and biblically-qualified leaders, Christ builds and grows his Church.

1. Jesus is the head of the Church, which is his body.

> And he put all things under his feet and gave him as head over all things to the church, which is his body, the fullness of him who fills all in all. **EPHESIANS 1:22–23**

Paul often used the analogy of a human body to describe the relationship between Jesus and the Church. As its head, Jesus is preeminent and has all authority to lead and govern the Church. As his body, the Church derives its life from his indwelling Spirit. The Church is his embodied presence in this world, called to do his work by serving others as his hands and feet.

Scripture uses other metaphors to describe the Church and its relationship to Jesus. As the bride of Christ, the Church is the beloved of Jesus, who laid down his life to redeem her for himself in an eternal covenant. As the family of God, the Church looks to Jesus as its elder brother, who exercises all the rights and privileges of God's firstborn Son in caring for his brothers and sisters. As God's holy priesthood, the Church serves under Jesus, the great high priest who sacrificially offered himself to reconcile lost and sinful people to God. Similarly, the Church is to offer spiritual sacrifices to God through Jesus as it serves his mission of reconciliation in the world. These metaphors and others provide a rich description of the Church's central place in God's heart and eternal plan.

The Church is his embodied presence in this world, called to do his work by serving others as his hands and feet.

Our love for the Church reflects our love for God. Jesus loved the Church so much that he shed his blood to save her. He did this before she was holy and blameless. We must grow to love the Church even in its imperfect condition, for Jesus values her with his own life. The one who mistreats her offends him, but the one who honors her receives his commendation as we look to the day when Jesus will present her to himself in glory.

2. The Church is universal and local.

Now to him who is able to do far more abundantly than all that we ask or think, according to the power at work within us, to him be glory in the church and in Christ Jesus throughout all generations, forever and ever. Amen. **EPHESIANS 3:20–21**

Paul prayed by the Spirit that one day all believers would be filled with the fullness of God. This must have sounded astonishing to the Ephesian believers until Paul explained how it would happen: God's power would bring it to pass. God would be glorified in his sinless Son through his Church for all generations.

God's Church is universal. It includes all who have been regenerated by the Spirit and believe Jesus is the sinless Son of God, crucified for our sins and raised from the dead. This universal Church includes all believers throughout time, whether now in heaven or on earth. But God's Church is also local. The New Testament refers to specific regional churches, city churches, and churches that met in homes in the early years after Jesus' resurrection. Yet not everyone who participates in a local church's activities is a member of God's universal Church. Only those in Christ belong to him and his Church, for Paul wrote, "The Lord knows those who are his" (2 Timothy 2:19).

Each of us who believes in Jesus is part of his universal Church. But that is not enough. God has called us to walk together in a local church with other believers. Only in the context of a local church can we live out many of the New Testament exhortations. Love, service, and spiritual growth happen in the context of mutually reciprocal relationships in a faith community. Loners cannot experience the fullness of the Christian life. Our fellowship with one another should imitate the relationship between the Father, the Son, and the Holy Spirit, for this Triune God calls us into fellowship with himself and one another.

3. The Church regularly and purposefully meets together.

And let us consider how to stir up one another to love and good works, not neglecting to meet together, as is the habit of some, but encouraging one another, and all the more as you see the Day drawing near. **HEBREWS 10:24–25**

The author of Hebrews was concerned that forces were tempting the believers to abandon their faith and commitment to Jesus. He urged them to continue to meet together and also to think about how they could use their meetings to encourage each other to keep growing in their love for God and one another. He wanted their gatherings to fuel their devotion to Christ and lead to good works in their lives.

Protestant churches have historically identified the following activities as essential to a true Church according to the New Testament. It is our love for God and others that should motivate these activities:

- Proclaim and worship Jesus.
- Administer water baptism and Communion.
- Correct doctrinal and moral faults.
- Train and disciple believers for the work of service.

The above activities require that we follow Jesus through active in-person participation in the local church. Participating in church online may temporarily supplement isolated situations, but it can never replace what God does when we gather together. For example, the nearly sixty specific commands in the New Testament concerning how we should relate to one another must be done in person. These commands are the basis for the Christian community and directly impact our witness to the world. Technology is an inadequate method for us to live these admonitions. We need the physical proximity that deepens our bonds to one another and helps anchor our commitment to God. Let us, therefore, prioritize our church meetings and consider how we can encourage and inspire one another to love God and be rich in good works.

4. Jesus builds the Church through the Holy Spirit.

While they were worshiping the Lord and fasting, the Holy Spirit said, "Set apart for me Barnabas and Saul for the work to which I have called them." **ACTS 13:2**

The book of Acts is Luke's report concerning Jesus' ongoing ministry through the Holy Spirit after his resurrection. He tells us that the Spirit empowered the early church to proclaim the good news and make disciples in all nations. Led by the Holy Spirit, Jesus' disciples spread the gospel from Jerusalem to nearby regions and eventually to the capital of the Roman empire. The text above recounts the significant moment when the Holy Spirit ordered the leadership of Antioch's multiethnic church to send two leaders on a mission to bring the gospel to new cities and regions.

The early church depended entirely on the Holy Spirit for its life and growth. The Spirit filled the disciples with his presence, empowered them, guided them, prophesied to them, emboldened them, performed healings and miracles through them, and added to their number. It was the normal experience of the early church for the Holy Spirit to manifest his presence among them. As Jesus taught and Paul confirmed, the Holy Spirit revealed divine truth to the churches so they might know God and his great salvation in Jesus Christ. Jesus said he would build a victorious Church, and he is doing it through the Holy Spirit.

We must reject the thought that we can build the Church simply by working hard. We must instead be as dependent on the Holy Spirit for the Church's health and growth as the first disciples were. Without him, we can do nothing of lasting value. With him, we can effectively preach the gospel, make disciples, and grow the Church. His life-giving presence and enabling power spur the Church's growth in maturity and salvations. Let us faithfully follow the Holy Spirit's direction so that we might be Christ's fruitful co-laborers in building his Church.

5. Jesus builds the Church through leaders and equipped believers.

> *And he gave the apostles, the prophets, the evangelists, the shepherds and teachers, to equip the saints for the work of ministry, for building up the body of Christ.* **EPHESIANS 4:11–12**

In chapters one through three of Paul's letter to the Ephesians, he elaborated on God's glorious destiny for the Church. In chapter four, he then explained how the Church would grow into maturity and fulfill this purpose through the spiritual leaders Jesus would give to the Church. God commissioned these leaders to equip believers to serve one another and build the Church. Speaking the truth in love and serving others well would cause the Church to grow and mature as it built itself up in love.

Jesus is the apostle, prophet, evangelist, shepherd, and teacher who knows how to care for and equip his Church.

Jesus is the apostle, prophet, evangelist, shepherd, and teacher who knows how to care for and equip his Church. He looks for men and women to fulfill these roles, people willing to pour their lives out in service to others. He calls and empowers faithful disciples to lead and equip the Church through his Spirit, giving them a portion of his ministry.

Likewise, he calls every believer to be equipped so they might walk in the good works he has planned for them. As Jesus demonstrated, these good works should accompany the Church's gospel proclamation. They are not just for the benefit of fellow believers.

We are all called to serve others in some way. Consequently, we must be spiritually equipped. We should learn how to communicate the gospel and help others begin to follow Jesus. This should include teaching them how to pray, read Scripture, and share their faith. We should also learn how to walk with the Holy Spirit to express spiritual gifts to serve others. Throughout our lives, we should be learning and growing in our capacity to serve as Christ's coworkers and the Holy Spirit's partners. Let us not shrink from spiritual responsibility but wholeheartedly pursue God's will for our lives.

MEMORY VERSE

And he put all things under his feet and gave him as head over all things to the church, which is his body, the fullness of him who fills all in all. **EPHESIANS 1:22–23**

Application Questions ✎

How could you increase your effectiveness in contributing to the Church's growth?

How have other people helped you grow as a follower of Jesus and a member of his Church?

How could you help others be restored to the Church or continue in the Church if they are drifting away?

Pray each day that the Holy Spirit would use you to minister to someone at your next Sunday worship service.

Discussion Questions

What does it mean for the Church to be the body of Christ? What are the implications?

|||||||||||||||||||||||||||||||||||||||||||||||||||||||||||||||||||||||||||||||||

Why is it essential for the Church to gather regularly in person?

|||||||||||||||||||||||||||||||||||||||||||||||||||||||||||||||||||||||||||||||||

What are some of the essential means by which the Church grows spiritually?

The Church's One Foundation

Written by Samuel Stone

The church's one Foundation
is Jesus Christ her Lord;
she is His new creation,
by water and the Word;
from heav'n He came and sought her
to be His holy bride;
with His own blood He bought her,
and for her life He died.

Elect from ev'ry nation,
yet one o'er all the earth,
her charter of salvation,
one Lord, one faith, one birth;
one holy Name she blesses,
partakes one holy food,
and to one hope she presses,
with ev'ry grace endued.

Tho' with a scornful wonder,
men see her sore oppressed,
by schisms rent asunder,
by heresies distressed,
yet saints their watch are keeping,
their cry goes up, "How long?"
And soon the night of weeping
shall be the morn of song.

The church shall never perish!
Her dear Lord, to defend,
to guide, sustain, and cherish,
is with her to the end;
tho' there be those that hate her
and false sons in her pale,
against the foe or traitor
she ever shall prevail.

'Mid toil and tribulation,
and tumult of her war,
she waits the consummation
of peace for evermore;
till with the vision glorious
her longing eyes are blest,
and the great church victorious
shall be the church at rest.

Yet she on earth hath union
with God the Three in One,
and mystic sweet communion
with those whose rest is won.
O happy ones and holy!
Lord, give us grace that we,
like them, the meek and lowly,
on high may dwell with Thee.

Samuel Stone (1839–1900) was born in the English Midlands at the rectory of his father's Anglican church. He trained for the ministry at Oxford and served several churches in the Greater London area.

In the early 1860s, an Anglican bishop in South Africa wrote a compelling challenge against the inerrancy of Scripture. When the South African church leaders deposed him, he appealed to the Anglican hierarchy in England. A controversy arose as a result, and Stone countered with twelve hymns on the articles of the Apostles' Creed. "The Church's One Foundation" was his response to the ninth article, "one holy catholic church."

Samuel Sebastian Wesley, the grandson of hymnodist Charles Wesley, composed the music to the song. Various publications have printed different versions of the verses.

YouTube

The Church's One Foundation

Indelible Grace

CHAPTER 10

The Doctrine of the
Sacraments

Lord, I am not worthy to be a guest at your holy table, yet I have heard the sweet words of your invitation. So, I come to the sacrament of your only-begotten Son, our Lord Jesus Christ. Grant that I may receive not only the sacrament of the body and blood of our Lord but also its full grace and power. As one sick, I come to the Physician of life; unclean to the Fountain of mercy; blind to the Light of eternal splendor; poor and needy to the Lord of heaven and earth. Therefore, through your infinite mercy and generosity, heal my weakness, wash my uncleanness, give light to my blindness, and clothe my nakedness. I receive Communion with reverence and humility, repentance and devotion, purity and faith, purpose and intention. I know your divine Word and promise are true, and I rest upon them.[1]

---

1 — Adapted from the prayer of Thomas Aquinas and the prayers of Martin Luther.

Jesus commanded us to participate in two sacraments, baptism, a one-time rite of initiation (Matthew 28:19, Galatians 3:27); and Communion, a continuous rite of remembrance (1 Corinthians 11:23–26). They are not just personal experiences but public events that join us in the community of believers and separate us from the world. The Westminster Confession says the sacraments' purpose is "to put a visible difference between those that belong to the church and the rest of the world (XXVII.1)."

Various parts of the Church have warred over the purpose and practice of the sacraments for two thousand years. This continual conflict is evidence of the sacraments' inestimable value because the Enemy always attacks the truth that is most harmful to his designs. This should warn us not to take lightly how important they are to our spiritual growth.

John Calvin committed significant time to discussing the sacraments in his *Institutes of the Christian Religion.*

John Calvin

John Calvin (1509–1564) experienced a sudden spiritual conversion while studying the arts and civil law as a teenager in Paris. He immediately turned his attention to Scripture and the teachings of the rising Reformation. But religious and academic leaders persecuted him for supporting the Reformation, and he fled Paris, eventually settling in Geneva in 1536. There he helped organize the Protestant church and the city's civil order. From Geneva, his ideas and practices spread to many nations, making him one of the most influential theologians and church reformers in church history.

Calvin was a prolific writer. At age twenty-six, he published the first edition of his *Institutes of the Christian Religion,* one of history's most significant literary and theological works. He continually refined it and published the final version in 1559.

In the *Institutes,* he asserted that a sacrament is a visible sign of an invisible grace—rejecting transubstantiation, which maintains the bread and wine of Communion become the literal flesh and blood of Christ. He argued that the Scriptures teach Christ is spiritually present when worshippers approach him in faith as they receive Communion. Therefore, Communion should spiritually strengthen believers in their relationship with Jesus, reaffirming his covenant with them. This view has significantly influenced the Church for the last five hundred years.

Title page from the final edition of Calvin's magnum opus, *Institutio Christiane Religionis.*

Portrait of John Calvin (1509–1564)

What do we believe about the sacraments?

We believe *that water baptism and Communion are the two sacraments ordained by Christ, visible signs of God's covenant of grace. Baptism is the sacrament of entrance into the Church by which believers publicly identify with the death, burial, and resurrection of Jesus. Communion is the sacrament whereby believers corporately remember Christ's body given and his blood shed for their forgiveness. Sacraments are means of grace in which God is present, affirming his promises represented by the visible signs.*

1. Jesus ordained two sacraments: water baptism and Communion.

> *And Peter said to them, "Repent and be baptized every one of you in the name of Jesus Christ for the forgiveness of your sins ... So those who received his word were baptized, and there were added that day about three thousand souls. And they devoted themselves to the apostles' teaching and the fellowship, to the breaking of bread and the prayers.* **ACTS 2:38–42**

Jesus instructed his disciples to practice the two symbolic rites of water baptism and Communion. Both are connected with his atoning death. Jesus himself submitted to baptism and presided over the institution of Communion at the Last Supper. His disciples were baptizing new followers under Jesus' direction before his crucifixion (John 3:22, 26; 4:1–2) and continued to baptize new believers after his resurrection. Likewise, the early disciples habitually partook of Communion as part of their church meals. Luke referred to it as the breaking of bread (Acts 2:42, 46).

Baptism has its roots in several sacred Jewish experiences and practices. By the time of Christ, Jewish priests and ordinary people passionate for

God practiced ceremonial washings symbolizing spiritual cleansing. New Testament authors correlated baptism with several events in redemption history, including:

- Israel's deliverance from Egypt's armies in the crossing of the Red Sea (1 Corinthians 10:1–2)
- Noah's deliverance from the catastrophic flood in the ark (1 Peter 3:20–21)
- Israel's practice of circumcision (Colossians 2:11–12)

Communion has its roots in the ceremonial use of bread and wine in the Passover meal, commemorating God's deliverance of Israel from Egypt when the blood of sacrificial lambs spared Israel's households from the avenging angel of death.

Jesus commands the practice of both sacraments. As Luke testifies in Acts, everyone who repented and believed was baptized. Likewise, the early church regularly received Communion together in their worship gatherings. Today, baptism should be one of the first acts of obedience to Christ, signaling a new believer's profession of faith in Jesus. Likewise, believers should regularly receive Communion to celebrate their crucified and resurrected Lord. Leading others to be promptly baptized after their confession of faith and habitually receive Communion will help them grow spiritually in their walk with Jesus.

2. In water baptism, believers identify with Jesus' death, burial, and resurrection.

> We were buried therefore with him by baptism into death, in order that, just as Christ was raised from the dead by the glory of the Father, we too might walk in newness of life. ROMANS 6:4

Paul wrote this letter to baptized Roman Christians to explain the significance of their experience, particularly as it related to Jesus Christ. Paul reminded them that their baptism was a baptism into Christ's death. Because the early church typically baptized people by immersing them in water, Paul used the language of resurrection to correlate Jesus' rising from the dead with their baptism experience of arising from the water. Jesus arose from the dead by the glory of the Father, and believers in Rome also rose to a new spiritual life in baptism.

In the Book of Acts, disciples baptized new believers as soon as possible after they repented and believed. Baptism was an act of faith, springing from the heart of someone who voluntarily repented and wanted to follow Jesus. Peter referred to it as a pledge of a good conscience toward God (1 Peter 3:21), meaning the believer promised to serve God faithfully.

By identifying with Jesus' death, burial, and resurrection in baptism, we signal our desire to die to sin and live for God. We also publicly display our belief that Jesus died for our sins and rose again to an immortal, indestructible, everlasting life on our behalf.

By identifying with Jesus' death, burial, and resurrection in baptism, we signal our desire to die to sin and live for God.

Water baptism was the typical way the early church added new believers, and it should be the same today. If you have not been baptized, you should do it as soon as possible in obedience to Christ. If you help someone come to faith in Jesus, you should instruct the new believer to be baptized as soon as possible.

3. In Communion, believers remember Jesus' atoning death.

The Lord Jesus on the night when he was betrayed took bread, and when he had given thanks, he broke it, and said, "This is my body, which is for you. Do this in remembrance of me." In the same way also he took the cup, after supper, saying, "This cup is the new covenant in my blood. Do this, as often as you drink it, in remembrance of me." **1 CORINTHIANS 11:23–25**

The Corinthian church was guilty of many sins, including violating one another by getting drunk and failing to share their food with the poor at their communal meals. To correct them, Paul reminded them that Jesus commanded his followers to receive the bread and cup as symbols of his body and blood, remembering what Jesus would do for them. He instructed them, above all things, to remember Jesus as they received Communion and to do it in a manner that would honor his sacrificial death.

We refer to Communion as the Eucharist—a term that means to give thanks. In Communion, we give thanks to God for Jesus' voluntary sufferings and death on our behalf. The bread represents his body, which he submitted to cruel torture by his persecutors even though he was innocent. The cup represents his blood, spilled unto death as he was horribly crucified to a tree and shamefully hung for all to see. He did this on our behalf so that he might forgive our sins.

We should remember Jesus' atoning death with humble, thankful hearts as we regularly receive Communion. And though Jesus' sufferings and death are deeply somber matters, we should also rejoice that God's love moved him to endure such a trial on our behalf. Communion reminds us of the penalty our sins deserve and God's love for us despite our condition. Because of this, we should experience Communion with great joy as we remember what Jesus did for us.

4. Sacraments are visible signs of God's covenant.

In him also you were circumcised with a circumcision made without hands, by putting off the body of the flesh, by the circumcision of Christ, having been buried with him in baptism, in which you were also raised with him through faith in the powerful working of God, who raised him from the dead. **COLOSSIANS 2:11–12**

Paul correlates water baptism with circumcision, which was a visible sign of God's covenant and promises to Abraham. Water baptism is a similar visible sign for the new covenant. The bread and cup of Communion also serve as visible signs of the new covenant, as reported by Luke when Jesus instituted the sacrament at the Last Supper (Luke 22:19-20). Just as he had done for Israel, God gave the Church visible signs to serve as reminders of his new covenant with his people, those who repent and trust in Jesus Christ.

Jesus fulfilled the requirements of the former

covenant on our behalf and was punished for our sins under the Law. By doing this, he instituted a new covenant in which God grants us his righteousness and the gift of the Holy Spirit. Consequently, God causes us to be regenerated to become new creatures in Christ. We experience new life based on a new covenant in Jesus Christ. Through him, all the promises of God are "yes" to us in the new covenant.

Every time a new believer is baptized or we take Communion, it reminds us of God's covenant with us, secured by Jesus' death, burial, and resurrection. The visible symbols of water, bread, and the cup remind us of the extraordinary sacrifice Jesus made so that we might enter into a living relationship with God based on a new covenant. This covenant grants us Jesus' righteousness, God's Spirit, the promises of God, and the hope of eternal life. Baptism and Communion are truly moments for joyful celebration.

5. Sacraments are a means of grace.

The cup of blessing that we bless, is it not a participation in the blood of Christ? The bread that we break, is it not a participation in the body of Christ? **1 CORINTHIANS 10:16**

Paul wrote that the cup and bread of Communion are a participation or fellowship in the blood and body of Christ. In his proclamation on Pentecost, Peter associated baptism with the forgiveness of sins (Acts 2:38). Both statements link a sacrament with the experience of God's new covenant blessings. The sacraments are not magical; they do not possess inherent power that impacts participants regardless of their devotion. They are means of grace appointed by God to impart spiritual blessings when we come to him with humility and faith.

The spiritual nature of sacraments is consistent with God's revelation of himself and the physical creation. For example, God put a tree of life in the Garden—the fruit of which could have imparted immortality to our first parents. There was nothing magical about the tree, but it was a physical representation of God's grace. The sacraments are likewise a visible, physical means by which God refreshes, renews, and strengthens us in our faith.

Therefore, we should expect to receive God's blessing when we participate in one of his ordained sacraments because they are symbolic and also a means of grace. They remind us of his forgiveness and impart spiritual life to us through Jesus Christ through the Holy Spirit. Though we may not always be immediately aware of God's presence and blessing when participating in a sacrament, we can be sure God is faithful to fulfill his word. He will draw near to us as we draw near to him.

MEMORY VERSE

We were buried therefore with him by baptism into death, in order that, just as Christ was raised from the dead by the glory of the Father, we too might walk in newness of life. **ROMANS 6:4**

Application Questions ✎

When were you baptized, and what was your experience? What would prevent you from being baptized as soon as possible if you have not been baptized?

How often do you receive Communion, and what are your expectations when you do?

What Scriptures would you use, and what would you say to persuade a believer to be baptized?

Read the following passages about the Last Supper to prepare yourself better to receive Communion. Reflect upon and compare these passages: Matthew 26:20–29, Mark 14:17–25, Luke 22:14–20, 1 Corinthians 11:17–34, 1 Corinthians 10:16–17.

Discussion Questions

What does it mean for the Church to be the body of Christ? What are the implications? How do the sacraments of baptism and Communion serve as signs of God's covenant with us in Christ?

In what way are the sacraments more than symbols of remembrance?

Why is it important for every Christian to participate in both sacraments?

The Bread of Life for All Is Broken

Written by Timothy Tingfang Liu
Translated by Walter Reginald Oxenham Taylor

The bread of life for all is broken.
Christ drank the cup on Golgotha.
God's grace we trust, and
spread with reverence
This holy feast, and thus remember.

Timothy Tingfang Liu (1891–1947) was a leading Chinese educator and author with degrees from Chinese and American universities.

In the early 1930s, missionaries anticipating a revival in China sought to create a musical resource for the new believers. Six denominations commissioned the Hymns of Universal Praise project to meet this need. Liu agreed to chair the committee but insisted that at least ten percent of the hymns were Chinese. He wrote this hymn in 1934 in Mandarin and included it in the Hymns of Universal Praise project.

The project editor, Bliss Wiant, stated that "Chinese Christians who were inmates of Japanese prison camps in the late 1930s and World War II, not being able to celebrate Holy Communion, would sing or chant in a call-and-response style this hymn of Christian unity on Christ's suffering, death, and promised presence."

YouTube

The Bread of Life for All Is Broken (Jiu Shi Zhi Shen)

CHAPTER 11

The Doctrine of
Sanctification

OPENING PRAYER

Jesus, you are the living Word, and your Word is truth. Your words are the power of God that changes us. Open our hearts by your Holy Spirit, that through the preaching of your Word we may grow daily in grace and holiness. Sanctify us with the Word of your holy gospel. Transform us into your image. Set us apart for your high and holy purpose of living in your kingdom. Let your Word expand in our hearts until we live according to your good and gracious will. Keep us steadfast in your grace and truth, protect us from all temptation, and direct our steps so that we may walk in holiness of heart and do what is good and well-pleasing in your sight.[1]

---

1 — Adapted from the sixteenth-century Saxon Agenda: Historic Collect for the Reformation, the Lutheran Hymnary, and the first-century prayers of Clement of Rome.

Sanctification is not an immediate event but an ongoing cooperative process. It is ongoing because it begins at conversion and continues until the day we die. It is cooperative because God has a part and we have a part. And it's a process because no one looks like Jesus at the moment of conversion. It takes time, effort, and massive quantities of grace to reflect a little of his likeness.

Conversion should invariably lead to changed behavior. If there is no change in the life and character of a person who has professed Christ, it is doubtful that the person has experienced a true conversion. Therefore, sanctification is the testimony that a work of grace has really happened in our hearts.

John Wesley was deeply concerned about this issue. He witnessed too many people profess faith in Christ but continue to live as if they did not have genuine faith. He often wrote and preached about sanctification.

John Wesley

On May 24, 1738, John Wesley recorded in his diary: "In the evening I went very unwillingly to a society in Aldersgate Street, where one was reading Luther's preface to Romans. About a quarter before nine, while he was describing the change which God works in the heart through faith in Christ, I felt my heart strangely warmed. I felt I did trust in Christ, Christ alone for salvation, and an assurance was given to me that he had taken away my sins, even mine, and saved me from the law of sin and death." Thus began the preaching ministry that would astound the nation and change the world.

Wesley (1703-1791) was the fifteenth child of Reverend Samuel and Susannah Wesley. He trained for the ministry at Oxford and became the leader of the "Holy Club," a group of devout students that included his brother Charles and

George Whitefield. After a failed ministry in the new colony of Georgia, he returned to London and soon had his conversion at Aldersgate.

But the Anglican clergy denied him the pulpit, so he took to the open fields after the example of Whitefield. For the next fifty-three years, he preached over 40,000 sermons and traveled over 250,000 miles on horseback. "The world is my parish," he said. He published 233 books and 5,000 tracts. At his death, over 500 preachers and 115,000 people called themselves Methodists.

His ministry focused on salvation and the holiness of heart and life that followed it. He believed genuine faith produced inward and outward purity. He despised the view that grace frees a believer from the obligation of obeying the moral law and called it the "worst of all heresies." "When the Holy Spirit infuses the grace of God into the soul, one's love for God and others is made pure, and their lifestyle must increase in virtue and loving, selfless actions."

Wesley's sanctification doctrines led to the nineteenth-century Holiness movement and eventually Pentecostalism and the Charismatic Movement in the twentieth century. The total current population of these churches is around 600 million—all indebted at some level to John Wesley.

John Wesley preaching on his fathers grave: in the church yard at Epworth Sunday, June 6, 1742.

What do we believe about sanctification?

We believe *that sanctification is the process, beginning at regeneration, whereby God conforms his people to the image of Christ through his Word and Spirit. By grace, Christians grow in holiness and love for God and others throughout their lives as they submit to Jesus, obey God's Word, and walk by the Spirit in fellowship with other disciples.*

1. God conforms believers to the image of Christ.

> *Now may the God of peace himself sanctify you completely, and may your whole spirit and soul and body be kept blameless at the coming of our Lord Jesus Christ. He who calls you is faithful; he will surely do it.* **1 THESSALONIANS 5:23–24**

Wayne Grudem defines sanctification as the "progressive work of God that makes us more free from sin and more like Christ in our actual lives."

Sanctification contrasts with justification. Justification is a one-time work of God that provides us with the legal standing of perfection in God's eyes. Therefore, the level of justification is the same in every believer. Justification is the work of God alone; we cannot justify ourselves. Martin Luther provided this illustration, "When we are justified, it is as though a doctor has just administered a sure and certain remedy for a fatal disease. Though the patient may still endure a temporary struggle with the residual effects of his illness, the outcome is no longer in doubt. The physician pronounces the patient cured even though a rehabilitation process must still be carried out."

If we continue Luther's metaphor, then the rehabilitation process is sanctification. Sanctification is not a one-time event like justification but one that is continuous throughout our lives. Therefore, every believer is at a different level of sanctification.

Sanctification is the work of God, but we must cooperate with him. Both parties have distinct roles in the process, with the goal being the image of Christ. God is at work in us to conform us to the image of his Son, and our confidence is in God's power to accomplish it. But we have an essential role to play in the process.

In the 1 Thessalonians passage, Paul emphasizes God's role in conforming us to the image of Christ. He has just finished a lengthy section concerning sexual purity, brotherly love, respect for leaders, love for other people, rejoicing, prayer, and concern for public worship. All of these are necessary for sanctification. But Paul identifies the power behind that process: God himself will sanctify you completely. He is faithful, and he will surely do it.

2. Believers grow in sanctification throughout their lives.

> *For just as you once presented your members as slaves to impurity and to lawlessness leading to more lawlessness, so now present your members as slaves to righteousness leading to sanctification.*
> **ROMANS 6:19**

Sanctification begins at regeneration. Theologians call this **Positional Sanctification**. It is the gift God gives us at conversion.

When we are born again, something significant changes in our lives. Many old sinful habits, patterns, and choices no longer control us. A definite break from the ruling power of sin and a reorientation of our desires from sin to righteousness occurs. A new spiritual life within controls us. This power keeps us from practicing sin, and we are no longer enslaved by it.

This is why the Bible occasionally refers to us as already sanctified. Paul said to the Ephesian elders, "I commend you to God and to the word of his grace, which is able to build you up and to give you the inheritance among all those who *are sanctified*." The Greek expression "are sanctified" implies a completed past activity and a continuing result. (See also 1 Corinthians 6:11.)

Sanctification increases throughout life.

Theologians call this **Progressive Sanctification**.

Sanctification should increase in our lives, but it rarely grows in a steady, upward direction. There are ebbs and flows throughout life. But the general trend should always be forward. "Not that I have already obtained this or am already perfect, but I press on to make it my own, because Christ Jesus has made me his own" (Philippians 3:12).

Sanctification is completed at death and when the Lord returns. Theologians call this **Perfect Sanctification**.

Although we can get increasingly more like Jesus, we will never be sanctified entirely in this life. John said, "We know that when he appears we shall be like him, because we shall see him as he is" (1 John 3:2). That knowledge produces in us a yearning for continuous sanctification. "And everyone who thus hopes in him purifies himself as he is pure" (1 John 3:3).

3. Believers grow in sanctification by grace.

> *Therefore, my beloved, as you have always obeyed, so now, not only as in my presence but much more in my absence, work out your own salvation with fear and trembling, for it is God who works in you, both to will and to work for his good pleasure.* **PHILIPPIANS 2:12–13**

The phrase "work out your own salvation" has created many misunderstandings throughout church history. Various religious traditions have claimed that it proves we must add works to our faith to attain salvation. But Paul does not say, "work for your salvation." He says, "work out your salvation." There is a vast difference between those two ideas.

The term "salvation" is a broad one encompassing everything God has done for us to deliver us from our lost condition in sin. It includes regeneration, justification, sanctification, adoption, and glorification. In this passage, sanctification is the emphasis.

Sanctification is a cooperative process, and our text underscores that idea. God works (as we saw in 1 Thessalonians 5:23–24), and we work. This does not mean we have equal roles in sanctification. Certainly, God's work is more significant. But it does mean that we have a role in the process. And that role is mainly a responsive one.

When Paul says God is at work in us, he uses a Greek word that conveys the idea of God actively and continually putting forth his energy to support and strengthen our obedience. The energy is his grace. It works on our will first, creating a holy desire to please God in all things. Then it energizes and motivates us to work for his good pleasure.

John Piper summarizes the power of grace to propel our sanctification this way: "The whole lifelong triumphant offensive called 'operation sanctification'—by which we wage war against all the remaining corruption in our lives—is sustained by the supply line of the Spirit that comes from the secure, unassailable home base of justification by faith alone. And it will be a successful operation—but only because of the unassailable home base."

4. Believers grow in sanctification with other believers.

May the Lord make you increase and abound in love for one another. . . . so that he may establish your hearts blameless in holiness before our God and Father, at the coming of our Lord Jesus with all his saints. **1 THESSALONIANS 3:12–13**

The New Testament regularly speaks of sanctification in the context of community. For example, Jesus petitioned the Father concerning his disciples: "Sanctify them in truth; your word is truth" (John 17:17), And then he prayed that "they may all be one, just as you, Father, are in me, and I in you, that they also may be in us . . . " (John 17:21). Jesus linked their growth in sanctification with their growth in their relationships with one another and himself and the Father.

In the 1 Thessalonians passage, Paul prays that the Thessalonian believers' love for one another would grow abundantly. As a result, God will establish their hearts blameless in holiness. When believers grow in their love for one another, they also grow in sanctification. At the end of the same letter, Paul prays again, "Now may the God of peace himself sanctify you [plural] completely . . ." (1 Thessalonians 5:23).

Paul's prayer for the entire Church comes after he has urged them to grow in their love for one another (3:12, 4:9), encourage one another (4:18, 5:11), build one another up (5:11), and do good to one another (5:15). Sanctification happens in community.

Paul exhorted Timothy to ". . . flee youthful passions and pursue righteousness, faith, love, and peace, *along with those who call on the Lord from a pure heart*" (2 Timothy 2:22; italics added). We flee evil and pursue sanctification with other Christians' aid.

The concept of our sanctification apart from the community of faith is a foreign concept to the New Testament. Sanctification requires community. We cannot become more like Jesus without walking in relationship with others.

5. Believers grow in sanctification through spiritual disciplines.

…train yourself for godliness; for while bodily training is of some value, godliness is of value in every way, as it holds promise for the present life and also for the life to come. **1 TIMOTHY 4:7–8**

The spiritual disciplines are scriptural practices designed to strengthen our relationship with God and make us like him. We can learn these activities and cultivate them through diligence, but like all training, they begin as a decision and should continue as a lifelong habit.

The disciplines are not means to attain righteousness; that is a gift from God. Instead, these activities are channels for God's power to transform us into his image. It is the Holy Spirit who initiates, energizes, and maintains the spiritual disciplines in our lives. However, he does it in partnership with our continuous choices to discipline ourselves. The disciplines can quickly degenerate into works for righteousness, but the Holy Spirit is a safeguard against that possibility.

There are many spiritual disciplines, but the main ones center around God's Word and prayer.

The Word of God is the primary instrument of sanctification. Jesus prayed that the Father

> *If we train ourselves for godliness through the spiritual disciplines, we will look more and more like Jesus daily.*

might "sanctify them in truth; your word is truth." Paul told the Ephesian church that Christ "gave himself up for her, that he might sanctify her, having cleansed her by the washing of water with the word." Peter told the scattered believers in Asia Minor that God's exceedingly great promises would make them "partakers of the divine nature, having escaped from the corruption in the world because of sinful desire."

Adding a disciplined life of prayer with the Word of God produces a powerful means of sanctification. Jesus told his disciples before he went to the cross, "Watch and pray that you may not enter into temptation. The spirit indeed is willing, but the flesh is weak" (Mark 14:38). The disciples saw the power of prayer in the life of Jesus, and they asked him to teach them to pray (Luke 11:1).

If we train ourselves for godliness through the spiritual disciplines, we will look more and more like Jesus daily.

MEMORY VERSE

Now may the God of peace himself sanctify you completely, and may your whole spirit and soul and body be kept blameless at the coming of our Lord Jesus Christ. He who calls you is faithful; he will surely do it. **1 THESSALONIANS 5:23–24**

Application Questions ✏️

How are your relationships with others aiding your sanctification? What practical steps could you take to increase that process?

What hindrances do you face that tend to hold you back from engaging in the kind of relationships that increase your sanctification? Why? What can you do to change?

Which spiritual disciplines do you find the most helpful in increasing your sanctification? Why?

Choose one area in which you need personal growth and focus your Bible reading and prayer on that area for the week.

Discussion Questions

What are some of the negative consequences of confusing justification with sanctification? How can you avoid them?

Putting too much emphasis on God's role in sanctification can result in spiritual apathy. Putting too much emphasis on our role in sanctification can result in moralism. Which tendency do you have? Why? What can you do to ensure you have the right balance?

Spiritual disciplines tend to devolve into legalistic duty. Why is that? How can you ensure that won't happen?

The Cleansing Wave

Written by Phoebe Worrall Palmer

Oh, now I see the crimson wave!
The fountain deep and wide;
Jesus, my Lord, mighty to save,
Points to His wounded side.

Refrain:
The cleansing stream I see, I see!
I plunge, and, oh, it cleanseth me!
Oh, praise the Lord, it cleanseth me!
It cleanseth me, yes, cleanseth me.

I see the new creation rise,
I hear the speaking blood;
It speaks, polluted nature dies,
Sinks 'neath the cleansing flood.

I rise to walk in Heav'n's own light,
Above the world and sin,
With heart made pure and garments white,
And Christ enthroned within.

Amazing grace! 'tis Heav'n below
To feel the blood applied,
And Jesus, only Jesus know,
My Jesus crucified.

Phoebe Worrall Palmer was born in 1807 to zealous Methodist parents who conducted family worship twice daily. She experienced a decisive move of the Holy Spirit at a Methodist revival in the 1830s and dedicated her life to advancing the gospel message of holiness.

In an age that frowned upon women preachers, she led weekly Bible studies, published books, and preached at hundreds of camp meeting revivals. Her prolific ministry earned her the title "Mother of the Holiness Movement Revival."

She was a link between John Wesley's revivalism and modern Pentecostalism. Her theology and legacy helped shape the Nazarenes, Salvation Army, Church of God, and Pentecostal-Holiness churches.

YouTube

The Cleansing Wave
Thomas Mayhew

CHAPTER 12

The Doctrine of the
Second Coming

OPENING PRAYER

The last promise you gave us in the Bible was, "Surely I am coming soon." In response to that promise, we say, "Amen. Come, Lord Jesus!" We long for that day when you will descend from heaven with a cry of command, with the trumpet of God, and the sound of a loud voice from the throne declaring, "Behold, the dwelling place of God is with man. He will dwell with them, and they will be his people, and God himself will be with them as their God. He will wipe away every tear from their eyes, and death shall be no more, neither shall there be mourning, crying, or pain, for you make all things new." Then you will take the power and the glory and claim the kingdom as your own. And every eye will see you, and those who have loved your appearing will receive the crown of righteousness.

Come, my Lord, no longer tarry and hasten the day when our faith shall be sight. When you come with shouts of acclamation, we shall bow in humble adoration and proclaim, my God, how great Thou art.[1]

---

1 — Adapted from various Bible texts and classic hymns.

The ultimate appearance of God's kingdom is the focus of the entire Bible, from Genesis to Revelation. But this scriptural emphasis is not on times, dates, or world events but on the revelation of Jesus Christ as the Sovereign Lord of all creation.

Christ's sacrifice on the cross secured our salvation and victory over sin and death. But his return will bring us to that state of complete victory when we have glorified bodies unstained by sin and fleshly desires. That will be the fulfillment of our blessed hope.

Christ's return is an event of such grandeur and awe that it has enticed men and women throughout history to speculate concerning the very thing Jesus said we could not know: the time and place of his return. Montanus was the first recorded example we have of this dangerous tendency.

Montanus

Around 156, a Christian named Montanus went into a trance and began prophesying in a small village in the Roman province of Phrygia. He claimed divine inspiration and actively recruited followers throughout Asia Minor. He claimed that he and his disciples were the last in a succession of prophets and that their mission was to prepare all believers for the heavenly descent of the New Jerusalem.

Montanus predicted the speedy return of Christ and gave the exact location of his arrival. He trained his followers to be an elite Christian minority preparing for the coming age by withdrawing from the world. He proclaimed a new era of prophecy and dubbed his group the "New Prophecy" movement. They won converts in Asia Minor, Rome, and other major cities.

Many church leaders feared the potentially divisive effects of the movement. In 192, the bishop of Antioch declared that "the working of the lying organization called the New Prophecy is held in abomination by the whole brotherhood in the

A Greek icon depicting the Second Coming, c. 1700.

world." Regional synods in Asia Minor convened to address the controversy and eventually excommunicated Montanus and his followers.

But there were a few orthodox leaders who did not condemn the movement. Irenaeus, the bishop of Lyon and second-century church father, thought that those attacking the Montanists would drive the authentic gift of prophecy from the Church. He thought Montanus' detractors were setting aside "both the gospel and the prophetic Spirit." The church father, Tertullian, joined the Montanists and wrote books defending them, although he eventually left the movement.

Montanus was the first recorded individual to predict the specifics of Christ's return, but he would not be the last. He provides an example of the foolishness of predicting what Jesus said we could not know. "But concerning that day and hour no one knows, not even the angels of heaven, nor the Son, but the Father only" (Matthew 24:36).

What do we believe about the second coming?

We believe *that Jesus, the King of kings and Lord of lords, will return to earth bodily, in power and glory, at a time fixed by the Father and unknown to the Church, to raise the dead and judge the world. He will clothe the righteous with immortal, glorious bodies, rewarding them according to their deeds. But the unrighteous, Satan, and the forces of darkness, he will punish with eternal destruction. God will consummate redemption and renew creation, and his people from every nation will enjoy, worship, and reign with him forever.*

1. Jesus will return to the earth bodily.

"This Jesus, who was taken up from you into heaven, will come in the same way as you saw him go into heaven." **ACTS 1:11**

God's rule is continuously advancing throughout history. It will culminate in the final establishment of his kingdom when Jesus returns to the earth suddenly, visibly, and bodily. He is the Sovereign Lord of creation and history, and when he returns to establish his kingdom, he will remove all evil and set up his throne of righteousness and justice. God is in control of history, and his victory is assured.

The theme of God's coming kingdom unfolds in Scripture from Genesis to Revelation. The biblical writers never emphasize times, dates, or world events but God's plan to establish his rule on earth. Therefore, we should look forward to the Lord's return, but we should not be consumed with dates and times. God has set a definite time for the return of Christ, but no man knows when it will be (Mark 13:32–33, 35).

One reason God has not told us when Jesus will return is so we will not turn our focus away from the Great Commission and toward self-preservation. Rather than being concerned with "when he will return," God wants us to focus on "why he will return." We should not wait passively for his return but actively obey the mandate to make disciples of all nations. God's victorious return should spur us to action as we disciple the nations.

But we do look forward to his return. Because he ascended with a physical body and will return with a physical body, we have hope that we will also have glorified physical bodies one day. This assures us that the material creation is valuable to God and is part of his ultimate plan for the universe. This knowledge protects us from asceticism—severe self-discipline and avoidance of all forms of indulgence. We can fully enjoy God's material blessings as a part of our worship.

2. Jesus will judge the world when he returns.

> *When the Son of Man comes in his glory, and all the angels with him, then he will sit on his glorious throne. Before him will be gathered all the nations, and he will separate people one from another as a shepherd separates the sheep from the goats.* **MATTHEW 25:31–32**

"He ascended into heaven and is seated at the right hand of the Father." The Apostles' Creed affirms the glorious truth that Christ has ascended into heaven and reigns victorious. It further affirms, "He will come again to judge the living and the dead." This truth stirs our hearts with the promise that every wrong will one day be made right. That should comfort us and terrify us at the same time.

Everyone will die and face a personal judgment of either damnation or salvation (Hebrews 9:27). There will be a great final judgment of believers and unbelievers. All will stand before the judgment seat of Christ and hear his proclamation of their eternal destiny. Life is not cyclical, and we do not get multiple chances through reincarnation. Death and judgment are the inevitable reality for all people.

This judgment is good news for Christians. For on that day, Jesus will say, "Come, you who are blessed by my Father, inherit the kingdom prepared for you from the foundation of the world"

(Matthew 25:34). But this judgment is bad news for unbelievers. For on that day, Jesus will say, "Depart from me, you cursed, into the eternal fire prepared for the devil and his angels" (Matthew 25:41).

This doctrine has several positive moral influences on our lives. It satisfies our inward need for justice. We live in a world marred by sin and rife with injustice, and we know that no laws or leaders can ultimately fix what is wrong. We long for the Judge of all the earth to do right (Genesis 18:25).

It also provides a motive for holy living and evangelism. Paul was deeply mindful of his accountability before a holy God. That knowledge produced in him the fear of the Lord, a yearning for holiness, and a desire to persuade others to reconcile with God. For we must all appear before the judgment seat of Christ, so that each one may receive what is due for what he has done in the body, whether good or evil. Therefore, knowing the fear of the Lord, we persuade others (2 Corinthians 5:10–11).

3. The righteous have a great hope in the resurrection.

> *Blessed be the God and Father of our Lord Jesus Christ! According to his great mercy, he has caused us to be born again to a living hope through the resurrection of Jesus Christ from the dead.* **1 PETER 1:3**

Jesus was raised from the dead on the third day, breaking death's hold on humanity. He is the "first-born from the dead" (Revelation 1:5, Colossians 1:18), "the firstfruits of those who have fallen asleep" (1 Corinthians 15:20). He was the first to

be resurrected eternally, but not the last. On the Final Day, God will raise the righteous to eternal life and the unrighteous to eternal condemnation (John 5:28–29, Daniel 12:2–3, Acts 24:15). So, his resurrection ensures our resurrection. It gives us a living hope, a hope that is securely kept for us in heaven. It is our inheritance, imperishable, undefiled, and unfading (1 Peter 1:4–5).

But though God purchased our salvation through his Son's death, our final salvation will not be complete until the "day of the Lord Jesus Christ." This is what theologians call the already, not yet tension. In this life, we experience his promises, but the full completion of those promises awaits our resurrection on the Last Day.

That is why Christianity is a forward-looking faith. It is a life of hope. The basis of our hope is the finished work of Jesus Christ, but the object of our hope is the final appearance and complete salvation he will bring when he returns. His sacrifice on the cross secured our salvation and victory over sin and death. But his return will bring us to that state of complete victory when we have our glorified bodies that are unstained by sin and fleshly desires.

Therefore, hope is our dominant perspective about the future. We are not simply trying to hold on until Jesus comes back; we labor expectantly during the brief time God enables us to inhabit his planet. And we labor against the backdrop of Christ's ultimate return in victory, power, and glory.

4. The wicked will pay the penalty of eternal destruction.

> ... when the Lord Jesus is revealed from heaven with his mighty angels in flaming fire, inflicting vengeance on those who do not know God and on those who do not obey the gospel of our Lord Jesus. They will suffer the punishment of eternal destruction, away from the presence of the Lord...
>
> **2 THESSALONIANS 1:7–9**

Jesus taught more about eternal judgment than any other biblical author. He called Hell a place of eternal torment (Luke 16:23) and unquenchable fire (Mark 9:43) from which there was no return (Luke 16:19–31)—a place of "outer darkness" (Matthew 25:30) where people will gnash their teeth in anguish and regret (Matthew 13:42). He called it Gehenna in reference to the valley along the south of Jerusalem where people burned garbage and corpses. Maggots consumed the bodies and the trash. Because there was a constant supply of trash and corpses, the maggots that fed on them "never died" (Mark 9:48).

Three Old Testament authors referred to eternal destruction: Daniel (12:1–2), Malachi (4:1), and Isaiah (66:22–24). Eight of the nine New Testament authors also referred to it: Matthew (18:8, 25:46),

Mark (9:48), Luke (3:17, 16:19–31), John (3:36), Paul (2 Thessalonians 1:7–9), Peter (2 Peter 2:4, 17), Jude (1:7, 13), and the author of Hebrews (9:27).

Despite all the biblical evidence, eternal destruction is still one of the most challenging doctrines to embrace. J. I. Packer said, "The sentimental secularism of modern Western culture, with its exalted optimism about human nature, its shrunken idea of God ... makes it hard for Christians to take the reality of Hell seriously. [It] assumes a depth of insight into divine holiness and human sinfulness that most of us do not have."[1]

God does not punish sinners in a fit of temper but rather as the result of his perfect love and unchanging hatred of evil. Hell is a place of justice, not cruelty. Cruelty involves punishment more severe than the crime. Cruelty, in this sense, is

---

1 — J.I. Packer, *Concise Theology: A Guide to Historic Christian Beliefs*

unjust, and God is incapable of inflicting an unjust punishment. But human concepts of justice and love are distorted by sin and, therefore, deceptive and unreliable. God is infinitely worthy of our love, obedience, and honor, and our failure to do so is an infinite evil and deserving of eternal destruction.

5. The entire creation will be made new and glorious.

Then I saw a new heaven and a new earth, for the first heaven and the first earth had passed away, and the sea was no more. **REVELATION 21:1**

"God created the earth ... to be man's permanent home. But sin and death entered the world and transformed the earth into a place of rebellion and alienation; it became enemy-occupied territory. But God has been working in salvation history to affect a total reversal of this evil consequence and liberate earth ... from bondage to sin and corruption" (Alan F. Johnson, *Expositors Bible Commentary*, 12:592).

Though God subjected the original creation to futility, the new creation will be free from corruption and full of the glory of God. Awaiting us is a glorious future kingdom where death is defeated, and God will wipe away tears of sorrow, pain, and grief. The sea—the source of the satanic beast (Revelation 13:1) and the place of the dead (Revelation 20:13)—will be no more. This is a symbolic picture of the new creation's freedom from evil in all its forms.

In this new creation, we will enter into the full enjoyment of life in the presence of God forever. Jesus will say to us, "Come, O blessed of my Father,

inherit the kingdom prepared for you from the foundation of the world" (Matthew 25:34). In this kingdom, "there shall no more be anything accursed, but the throne of God and of the Lamb shall be in it, and his servants shall worship him" (Revelation 22:3).

God made the original physical creation "very good" (Genesis 1:31). Nothing is inherently sinful about the physical world. God will perfect his creation in the new heavens and earth and bring it into harmony with his original purpose. We will dwell in a fully redeemed universe that is "very good."

We shall eat and drink at "the marriage supper of the Lamb" (Revelation 19:9). The "river of the water of life" will flow from the throne of God (Revelation 22:1). The tree of life will bear "twelve kinds of fruit for the healing of the nations" (Revelation 22:2). And our physical bodies will again be "very good" in God's sight to fulfill the purpose for which he created us. This is our blessed hope.

MEMORY VERSE

Blessed be the God and Father of our Lord Jesus Christ! According to his great mercy, he has caused us to be born again to a living hope through the resurrection of Jesus Christ from the dead, to an inheritance that is imperishable, undefiled, and unfading, kept in heaven for you, who by God's power are being guarded through faith for a salvation ready to be revealed in the last time. **1 PETER 1:3–5**

Application Questions ✎

Some believers are fascinated by the second coming and the possibility of his impending return. Others are confused by it and deliberately avoid the subject. What is your tendency? Why? Do you think you have a balanced approach?

What emotions do you feel when you contemplate Jesus judging the earth? Why?

If you believe the creation is good, how should that affect your life and mission?

Read a commentary on 1 Thessalonians 4:13–5:11 this week. Meditate on the practical application of Christ's return to your personal life.

Discussion Questions

Why is it important to embrace the doctrine of Hell and eternal judgment? What are the consequences if we do not? Is the doctrine difficult for you to embrace? What is it that makes it so difficult?

Large sections of the Church have historically tended to view the physical world as evil. What are the negative consequences of that view?

Does the return of Christ have 1) little effect on your daily life, 2) some effect on your daily life, or 3) a significant effect on your daily life? Why?

Swing Low, Sweet Chariot

Unknown Origin

Swing low, sweet chariot
Coming for to carry me home
Swing low, sweet chariot
Coming for to carry me home

I looked over Jordan and what do I see
(Coming for to carry me home)
A band of angels coming after me
Coming for to carry me home

If you get there before I do
(Coming for to carry me home)
Tell all my friends I'm coming too
Coming for to carry me home

Fisk Jubilee Singers, 1875

Shortly after the American Civil War, the president of Fisk University in Nashville sent a team of vocalists to tour the United States and Europe to raise funds for his struggling university. During their tour, the Fisk Jubilee Singers encountered the songs of Wallace Willis, a Choctaw Indian and former enslaved person. Wallace and his wife claimed to be the authors of the songs, but it is more likely they had heard them sung on the plantations of the Old South. The Fisk Jubilee Singers added "Swing Low, Sweet Chariot" to their repertoire and eventually recorded it. It gradually rose to international prominence and is now one of the world's most recognized hymns.

The songs of enslaved people in the American South were traditionally call-and-response songs that used repetition, powerful imagery, and a free-form structure to encourage continual adaptation and improvisation. The themes of resurrection and the glory to come resonated in them. This provided comfort and hope to a people doomed to a life of struggle and sorrow.

YouTube

Swing Low, Sweet Chariot
Etta James

Our Statement of Faith

Every Nation is a global family of campus-reaching churches. Founded in 1994, it exists to honor God and establish Christ-centered, Spirit-empowered, socially responsible churches and campus ministries in every nation.

Every Nation is also a member of the World Evangelical Alliance (WEA), a global network of evangelical churches and organizations. As a member, Every Nation adheres to the WEA's statement of faith.

As Every Nation's work expanded around the world, leaders recognized the need to better articulate its theological convictions and provide a solid foundation for its beliefs, practices, and mission in the world. In November 2022, Every Nation's Apostolic Council adopted Every Nation Seminary's Statement of Faith as Every Nation Churches & Ministries' Statement of Faith. In addition to adhering to the Apostles' Creed, the Nicene Creed, and the Chalcedonian Creed, Every Nation churches and campus ministries affirm and uphold the following articles of faith without reservation.

God

We believe in one God, creator and sustainer of all things. He is perfect and unchanging; completely loving, good, and holy; limitless in knowledge, power, and presence. God eternally exists in three persons: Father, Son, and Holy Spirit; one in essence, having the same divine attributes and perfections, with each person fulfilling distinct roles. Gracious in his eternal purpose to redeem a people for himself, God is worthy of wholehearted love and worship.

Scripture

We believe God has spoken through human authors in the Scriptures, the sixty-six canonical books of the Old and New Testaments. The Bible is the only written, verbally inspired Word of God and is self-attesting, unchanging, and without error in all it affirms. As God's authoritative, infallible, and sufficient revelation for life, doctrine, and practice, the Bible is to be trusted and obeyed.

Creation and Fall

We believe God created all things, visible and invisible, out of nothing, and all very good. He sovereignly sustains and governs creation for his glory and the benefit of his creatures. God created humans in his image, male and female, to know, love, and glorify him in covenant relationship and to serve as stewards of the earth. The first man, Adam, sinned against God, resulting in alienation, death, guilt, shame, and a curse upon the earth. Separated from God and subject to his judgment, all humans have inherited a sinful nature from which they cannot save themselves.

Jesus

We believe in Jesus Christ, the eternal Son of God, incarnated for our redemption, born of the virgin Mary, fully God and fully man, one person in two natures. As our substitute, he lived a sinless life and willingly gave himself as a propitiatory and reconciling sacrifice for our sins on the cross. He died, was buried, rose bodily on the third day, ascended into heaven, and sits at the right hand of God the Father as the only mediator between God and humanity. One day he will return again to judge the living and the dead.

The Gospel

We believe the gospel is the good news that God became man in Jesus Christ to reconcile lost people to himself. He lived a perfect, sinless life on our behalf and died on the cross for our sins. He was buried, and on the third day rose from the dead, securing our redemption forever. Having triumphed over Satan and the forces of darkness, he ascended into heaven as Lord of all. Everyone who repents and believes in him receives forgiveness of sins and eternal life.

Salvation

We believe that salvation, planned in eternity and promised throughout Scripture, is God's gracious act of rescue whereby he delivers lost and sinful people through faith in Christ's redemptive work. Because of his great love, God makes people spiritually alive in Christ through regeneration by the Holy Spirit. By grace, God forgives and justifies people through faith, apart from works, conferring upon them all the benefits of union with Christ, including the gift of God's righteousness, the indwelling Holy Spirit, and adoption into his family.

The Holy Spirit

We believe in God the Holy Spirit, giver and renewer of life, sent to guarantee our promised future. The Spirit convicts concerning sin, enlightens to the truth, awakens to repentance and faith, regenerates sinners, and unites believers to Christ, making them partakers of the divine nature. By the Spirit's indwelling, Christians enjoy God's presence and fellowship. By being filled with the Holy Spirit, Christians are divinely empowered for witness and ministry. As they bear the fruit of the Spirit and exercise spiritual gifts, believers edify the Church and bear witness to God's kingdom.

Missions

We believe God's mission is to redeem a people for himself from every tribe, nation, and language and to restore creation for his glory. As the Father loved the world and sent his Son, and the Father and the Son sent the Spirit, the Triune God sends the Church into the world to proclaim the gospel, make disciples, and seek God's justice and reconciliation in the world.

The Church

We believe in one holy, universal, and apostolic Church, the body of Christ of which Jesus is the head. As God's holy people on mission, the visible Church is expressed in gathered communities where believers assemble to pray, worship, hear God's Word, receive the sacraments, and fellowship with one another. Through the ministry of his Spirit, faithful disciples, and biblically-qualified leaders, Christ builds and grows his Church.

Sacraments

We believe that water baptism and Communion are the two sacraments ordained by Christ, visible signs of God's covenant of grace. Baptism is the sacrament of entrance into the Church by which believers publicly identify with the death, burial, and resurrection of Jesus. Communion is the sacrament whereby believers corporately remember Christ's body given and his blood shed for their forgiveness. Sacraments are means of grace in which God is present, affirming his promises represented by the visible signs.

Sanctification

We believe that sanctification is the process, beginning at regeneration, whereby God conforms his people to the image of Christ through his Word and Spirit. By grace, Christians grow in holiness and love for God and others throughout their lives as they submit to Jesus, obey God's Word, and walk by the Spirit in fellowship with other disciples.

The Second Coming

We believe that Jesus, the King of kings and Lord of lords, will return to earth bodily, in power and glory, at a time fixed by the Father and unknown to the Church, to raise the dead and judge the world. He will clothe the righteous with immortal, glorious bodies, rewarding them according to their deeds. But the unrighteous, Satan, and the forces of darkness, he will punish with eternal destruction. God will consummate redemption and renew creation, and his people from every nation will enjoy, worship, and reign with him forever.

GENERAL EDITOR

Steve Murrell is the cofounder and president of Every Nation Churches & Ministries, the founding pastor of Victory Church Manila, and a professor of Pastoral Theology at Every Nation Seminary. He earned a D.Min. from Asbury Theological Seminary and has authored six books. Steve and his wife, Deborah, have three sons, three daughters-in-law, and nine grandchildren. He loves two-wheel therapy on his Indian Chief Vintage motorcycle and whatever sports or arts his grandkids are doing.

CONTRIBUTORS

Paul Barker is a teacher and author who has served as a pastor and missionary. He also serves as a preaching coach for Every Nation Seminary and is one of the main instructors for Leadership 215. Paul and his wife, Aleta, have four grown children and ten grandchildren. He loves visiting art galleries and gardens with his wife, the St. Louis Cardinals, and anything related to England.

Bruce Fidler is the global manager for Leadership 215. He was born and raised in Germany and became a Christian at university. Since 1983, he has planted churches, led campus and international student ministry, and taught internationally. He is currently a PhD candidate and a Greek professor at Regent Seminary. He and his wife, Carol, live in Franklin, Tennessee, and have two adult sons. He loves family, friends, learning, and Liverpool F.C.

Tom Jackson is the senior pastor of Centrepoint Church in Scotland and serves on the Every Nation Europe Leadership Team. He holds a PhD from the University of Manchester, directs the Every Nation School of Ministry in Europe, and is the professor of Theology and Mission at Every Nation Seminary. He and his wife, Jean, have six daughters and two grandsons. He loves the North Carolina mountains, Ukrainian shashlik, and watching quirky television with his wife.

William Murrell is the academic dean and professor of Church History at Every Nation Seminary. Born and raised in the Philippines, William has graduate degrees in history from the University of Oxford (MSt) and Vanderbilt University (PhD) and teaches and writes on the history of missions and Muslim-Christian relations. William and his wife, Rachel, have a daughter and three sons. He loves old books, church architecture, and gardening with his wife and kids.